Modern Indian Fiction

Modern Indian Fiction

History, Politics and Individual in the Novels of Salman Rushdie Amitav Ghosh Upamanyu Chatterjee

P. S. RAVI

PRESTIGE

Published by
Prestige Books
3/28, East Patel Nagar
New Delhi 110 008

Printed at Chaman Offset Press, New Delhi 110 002

Contents

Preface

The efforts of several generations of writers—stretching from Bankim Chandra Chatterjee in the 1860s to Mulk Raj Anand, Raja Rao, R.K. Narayan to the experimental duo of G.V. Dasani and Arun Joshi in the 1960s—have attained a triumphant climax in the outburst of vibrant new talents in the 1980s and 1990s. With the publication of *Midnight's Children* the Indian English Novel has finally established its credentials, paving the way for a set of novels with similar preoccupations. Rushdie's experiment opened the floodgates for Amitav Ghosh and Upamanyu Chatterjee who in many ways imitated him. They form a trinity which heralded the Eighties novel.

Despite the breakthrough the critical attention which the novel of the Eighties has attracted is incomplete and at times unsatisfactory. Salman Rushdie with his unbridled talent has dominated this critical scenario, overshadowing the substantial contribution of his contemporaries Amitav Ghosh and Upamanyu Chatterjee. This book rose from the need to study these authors not as writers possessing individual talents but functioning as a group and representing a radically new phase in the development of the Indian English novel. This approach might be helpful in providing a totality of perception of the nature and significance of the novel of the Eighties. The novel of the Eighties has evolved from a new ethos, a transformed sensibility and startlingly original perspective. This book has chosen to study selected novels of three authors, Salman Rushdie, Amitav Ghosh and Upamanyu Chatterjee. The novels chosen for study are Salman Rushdie's *Midnight's Children* and *Shame*, Amitav Ghosh's *The Circle of Reason* and *The Shadow Lines* and Upamanyu Chatterjee's *English, August: An Indian Story*. The texts chosen do not merely belong chronologically to the Eighties by virtue of their dates of publication, they represent the principal features of the new genre. This study comprising five chapters deals with the significant changes from two aspects—the thematic and technical.

In Chapter One, the origin, growth and the development of the Indian English novel have been discussed. It has been shown how the Eighties novel is radically different from its predecessors. This chapter ends with the emergence of Salman Rushdie, Amitav Ghosh and Upamanyu Chatterjee on the literary scene.

Chapter Two, 'History, Politics and the Individual', commences the thematic study with a discussion of the dynamic interaction between History, Politics and the Individual. The novel of the Eighties gives a new perspective by its refreshing approach to the subject. The three novelists Salman Rushdie, Amitav Ghosh and Upamanyu Chatterjee, in spite of their pre-occupations with contemporary issues, still find it imperative to recapitulate the history of the past in their novels. This recapitulation serves to propound the new theory advocated by the novel of the Eighties. These novelists, particularly Salman Rushdie, regard individuals as being linked to history in three ways—History-bearing, History-suffering and History-creating. This chapter has been divided into three sections to depict the three facets. Incidents pertaining to the 'pre-Independence' era from all the five novels have been brought under the section pre-Independence to show the individual as History bearing. In a similar exercise the section entitled 'Partition' shows the individual as History-suffering. The third section 'post-Independence' diffuses the myth of history as Juggernaut. The individual is projected in a hitherto unexplored role as attempting to create history.

Chapter Three 'The Search for Identity' deals with the theme of the search for identity of the protagonists in the five novels against the background of the new cosmopolitanism and the increasing complexity of life in the sub-continent.

The protagonists of *Midnight's Children*, *Shame*, *The Circle of Reason*, *The Shadow Lines* and *English August: An Indian Story* have been shown to pass through three distinct phases in the course of their search for identity. Each phase traces a definite movement with the third phase proving the most decisive in the search.

Chapter Four analyses the innovative techniques used by the novelists. It studies how the realistic mode can no longer serve the purpose of the novel. The increasing complexities of modern life have forced the novelists to give the narrative a new structure. The new novel interfaces the oral narrative structure with various post-modernist techniques. Episodicity, story within story, fantasy, myth, magic realism, cinematic techniques and the new vibrant usage of the English language all combine to give the novel of the Eighties an unusual novelty.

In chapter five, the discussion is rounded off with a summary of observations made in the course of the book. Since the novelists under discussion are contemporaries and their writings too recent to have benefitted from extended critical discussion, any comment that has been made is at best tentative, not conclusive. These new novelists have taken the novel forward by continuing the tradition and going beyond it. The present study has aimed to place the Indian English novel of the Eighties in a critical perspective and indicate the significance of this writing in formulating an emerging consciousness.

Finally, I would like to express my deep gratitude to Professor M. Kumaraswamy Raju for his scholarly guidance in the preparation of this project; to Smt. Anuradha Roy for her suggestions and encouragement throughout the writing of this book; to Professor C.D. Narasimhaiah for allowing me to use the library at Dhvanyaloka, Mysore; to Sri Kubendra, Sri Deepak, my son Rohit, my nephew Siddarth for helping me in getting the book ready for print; to my father-in-law Sri Ramachandra Pillai for encouraging me to take up this research work; to my mother and wife for their active support and warm encouragement throughout this research project.

Origin, Growth and Development of Indian English Novel

The genesis of all literature lies in the instinctive human urge to express the drama of human experience. It was this urge which gave rise to the oral narrative tradition across the globe. With the growing sophistication of the written medium, the same urge found a more complex, subtle and fuller expression in formal literature. The development of the Indian English novel provides an interesting illustration of how this urge to express has taken a genre from the earliest phase of imitation through an intermediary phase of assimilation to reach a phase of authentic self-expression.

The novel as a literary phenomenon took roots in India a little more than a century ago. The development of formal prose began with the western impact on Indian culture. As a result, western classics were at the outset translated. A little later, followed works which were either imitations or inspired by western models. The novel proper begins with Bankim Chandra Chatterjee's first published work in English *Rajmohan's Wife* in the year 1864. It was a significant start for the Indian English novel. The presence of mystery and suspense casts it in the mould of romantic novels.. Bankim Chandra was a master of the romantic as well as the historical novel. But at the same time he was no stranger to comedy or humour either. His novels *The Poison Tree* and *Krishnakanta's Will* deal with social problems, a recurrent theme in Indian fiction. It is quite evident that his historical novels were inspired by Scott's historical romances. His chief pre-occupation is with patriotism, thus making the novel a means of political education. Bankim Chandra Chatterjee is rightly considered the father of the novel in India. Krishna Kripalani is right when he estimates the role played by Bankim Chandra

Chatterjee: "It was Bankim Chandra who established the novel as a major literary form in India. He had his limitations, he too was romantic, effusive and indulged a little too freely in literary flashes and bombast and was no peer of his great contemporaries, Zola and Dickens, much less of Tolstoy and Dostoevsky. There have been better novelists in India since then, but they all stand on Bankim's shoulders."[1]

Other writers too took the lead and started producing novels in English. Notable among them were Rajalakshmi Devi's *The Hindu Wife* (1876), Toru Dutt's *Bianca* (1878), Kali Krishna Lahiri's *Roshinara* (1881), H. Dutt's *Bijoychand* (1888) and Kshetrapal Chakravarti's *Sarata and Hingana.* K.R. Srinivasa Iyengar's remark that these novels "have for us today no more than an antiquarian or historical interest"[2] may not be acceptable as they played a vital role in quickening the literary renaissance all over the country.

The next important figure on the literary scene was Rabindranath Tagore. He came like a colossus on the Indian literary scene. He exerted a tremendous influence on the minds of the people with the choice of his themes. Tagore started by first imitating Bankim Chandra Chatterjee, till he found his own voice with *Choker Bali*. To Tagore goes the credit of nurturing the infant genre at its most important stage of growth. He brought a new force into the form as embodied in *Gora, The Home and the World, Binodini, The Wreck, Four Chapters* and *Farewell My Friend.* A significant fact of the period was that with Tagore, the growth of the Indian English novel and novels in regional languages in India developed almost on parallel lines. Tagore's novels helped the Indians to rediscover themselves and also created a new awareness about their culture. Tagore translated some of his Bengali works into English which helped in laying the foundations of the Indian English novel. His novels are mostly novels of ideas. He adapted the novel genre to depict the inner changes in the lives of characters in relation to time and space. Tagore's influence is all pervading, as can be seen in the novels of his successors Mulk Raj Anand, R.K. Narayan and a score of others. Sarat Chandra and Premchand carried the novel a little further by extending its range. Their preoccupation is with the downtrodden and the destitute. Their realistic and bold depiction of the misery of the lower classes foreshadows the best fiction of Mulk Raj Anand in English.

The arrival of Gandhi on the national scene in the 1920s galvanized the nation into tremendous activity. Gandhi's inspiring leadership turned the independence movement from a merely political struggle into an emotional experience. Commenting on the independence movement, Meenakshi Mukherjee says, "It was an emotional as well as an ideological experience spread over a much longer period of time than any other nationalist movement in history."[3] The coming of Gandhi did not only set the political scene alight but the literary scene also erupted into tremendous activity. Simultaneously, regional literatures too played a prominent part in shaping the sensibility of the Indian English Novel. The arrival of Mulk Raj Anand, Raja Rao, and R.K. Narayan, aptly termed 'the founding fathers' by William Walsh, on the literary scene gave the Indian English novel a new vigour and direction. Commenting on their decisive contribution, William Walsh says that the three writers are "distinguished not only for their own work but as the inaugurators of the form itself since it was they who defined the area in which the Indian novel in English was to operate, drew the first models of its characters and themes and elaborated its particular logic. Each used his own version of an English freed from the foggy taste of Britain."[4]

Another significant development with the advent of Gandhi on the political scene was the middle class taking an avid interest in creative writing, which earlier had been the monopoly of the upper classes. Ordinary people suddenly found that their own lives could be made the theme of literature. To quote M.K. Naik on the subject: "It is no mere coincidence that there came a sudden flowering of Indian fiction in the 1930s—a period during which the star of Gandhi attained the meridian on the Indian horizon. Under the leadership of Gandhi, the Indian struggle for freedom, already more than a generation old, became so thoroughly democratised that the freedom consciousness percolated, for the first time, to the very grass roots of Indian society, and revitalized it to the core. It is possible to see a close connection between the growth of nationalist consciousness and the development and rise of the Indian novel in English. Fiction, of all literary forms, is most vitally concerned with social conditions and values, and at that time, Indian society, galvanized into a new social and political awareness, was bound to seek creative expression for its new consciousness and the novel has in all ages been a handy instrument for this purpose."[5]

The writers were quick to respond to Gandhi's call. However, the handling of the theme depended on the writers' individual perceptions and sensibilities. Novels like K.S. Venkataramani's *Kandan the Patriot*, Raja Rao's *Kanthapura*, Mulk Raj Anand's *The Sword and the Sickle*, *Untouchable* and *Coolie* were novels written during the storm and stress of the freedom movement. There were also novels that took up this theme after independence like Khwaja Ahmed Abbas's *Inquilab* (1955), Manohar Malgonkar's *A Bend in the Ganges* (1964), R.K. Narayan's *Waiting for the Mahatma* (1955), Nagarajan's *Chronicles of Kedaram* (1961), Nayanatara Sahgal's *A Time to be Happy* (1952) and Bhabani Bhattacharya's *Shadow from Ladakh* (1966). In all these novels Gandhi is depicted as a multidimensional force. He appears directly as a character in some novels or as a driving force represented by an idealised character. The Gandhian theme of 'Back to the villages' and the struggle for freedom found eloquent artistic expression in K.S. Venkataramani's *Murugan the Tiller* and *Kandan the Patriot*. These novels created a sensation in the thirties. As K.R. Srinivasa Iyengar says, "Kandan gained in importance because it was the very image of the excruciating times we were passing through."[6] Venkataramani himself had introduced *Kandan the Patriot* as a novel of new India in the making and dedicated it to the unknown volunteers in India's fight for freedom. His other novel *Murugan the Tiller* spreads the Gandhian message of economic emancipation of the poor. Raja Rao strongly identifies himself with the Gandhian movement, and gives it passionate expression in his novel *Kanthapura*. *Kanthapura* covers the movement of Gandhi in the 1920s, and ends with the Gandhi-Irwin pact of 1931. Choosing a garrulous old woman as his storyteller, Raja Rao uses a small village as a symbolic representation to depict the gathering storm on the political horizon. Moorthy the protagonist is a Gandhian in both thought and principle. The trials and tribulations of the simple villagers participating in the freedom struggle are captured vividly, with the description alternating between the serious and the comic. The flexible pattern of the novel gives the novelist the room to weave together the allied threads of the Gandhian revolution, such as propaganda against evils of drinking, exploitation of coolies, the evils of superstition and other social evils. C.D. Narasimhaiah aptly sums up the focus of *Kanthapura* when he says, "The entire action [in the novel] comes out as an artist's enactment of Nehru's image of the impact of Gandhi on the Indian scene together with a hundred particulars that illuminated many hidden spots in the life of the country during that period."[7] Inspired by Gandhi, Mulk Raj Anand wrote *Untouchable* in which he highlights the age-old evil of segregation of an entire group of society based on their profession, a problem against which Gandhi fought all his life. In his other novel *Coolie*, Anand presents the world of proletarian misery and wretchedness. Anand's subtle strokes and the intensity with which he projects his protagonist Munoo, has put the young hero on par with some of the heroes of the novels of Charles Dickens. His third novel in the trilogy *The Sword and the Sickle* introduces Gandhi as a character. The novel deals with the peasant boy Lal Singh being taken from his North I[illegible] lage and a life stifled by suffocating layers of custom and religion, into the ferocity of the great war in Europe and then back to India and a new political awakening. The novel traces the development of Lalu against the background of the developing political situation. Events are represented through the protagonist Lalu's consciousness.

In the novels written on the same theme after Independence, there is a certain amount of distancing. *Inquilab* by K.A. Abbas is an important novel which falls into this pattern. Gandhi appears in person in this novel. The protagonist Anwar is shaped directly by the forces of history. Events of national importance are presented through the point of view of a young man who grows up and comes to maturity in the third decade of the century, the hub of the freedom movement. Anwar forms the central consciousness of the novel; his development is determined by events of national importance. All the major political incidents between Jallianwala Bagh and the Gandhi-Irwin Pact are brought into focus by involving the protagonist in each crisis. Manohar Malgonkar's *A Bend in the Ganges* is panoramic in scope and epical in aspiration. It is crowded with events from modern Indian history, beginning with the Civil Disobedience movement of the Thirties and ending with the post-partition riots in the Punjab. It captures the human drama against the background of a crowded national calendar. R.K. Narayan deals with the Gandhian theme for the first time *in Waiting for the Mahatma.* The novel introduces Gandhi as a person and not as a symbol. Gandhi's presence in this novel is not remote and does not border on the supernatural. He is rather presented as a warm human being who touches two young lives and transforms them. There is a marked difference in the handling of the theme in these later novels. A certain amount of detachment creeps into the narrative, as the experience is not immediate. Significantly, in these novels, Gandhi is humanised and is not an awe-inspiring figure anymore. The point of focus here is more on the human relationships rather than the historical struggle. Commenting on this difference, Meenakshi Mukherjee says:

> In these novels written in Nineteen Fifties which deal with the same theme, a noticeable distance between the author and the events has crept in, although this does not necessarily result in a better artistic realisation of the theme. In *Waiting for Mahatma* and *Chronicles of Kedaram*, the novelists are detached enough from the course of history to treat Gandhi casually as a human being or an idea rather than as an overwhelming symbol, and concentrate on weaving stories of human relationships which only marginally touch upon the struggle.

After a bitter and prolonged struggle India did get her freedom finally in 1947. However, a pall of gloom encircled the celebration of freedom, as the partition perpetrated on the country took its full toll. Serious writers now turned their attention to give expression to the partition carnage. Commenting on the subject K.R. Srinivasa Iyengar says, "After the advent of freedom, the more serious novelist has shown how the joy of freedom has been neutralized by the tragedy of partition."[9] Khushwant Singh's *Train to Pakistan*, Chaman Nahal's *Azadi*, Raj Gill's *The Rape*, Bonophul's *Betwixt Dream and Reality*, Padmini Sengupta's *Red Hibiscus* are novels which try to capture the shock and misery of a people who suddenly found themselves belonging to two countries.

The earliest novel on the theme of partition was Khushwant Singh's *Train to Pakistan* (1956). It deals with the eruption of violence between the Sikhs and the Muslims in a small village Mano Majra along the newly established Indo-Pakistan border. The carnage is seen through the eyes of the Sikh and Muslim community, who in spite of having lived peacefully together for several centuries, suddenly turned enemies. Paradoxically, Khushwant Singh has used all his imaginative power to present a truthful picture. The result is that the horrors of partition are exposed in all their stark nakedness. William Walsh comments, "The objectivity, detachment and impartiality makes the horrors it describes . . . with all their madness and ferocity all the more convincing, all the more devastating. There is no merciful mist shrouding these accurately reported calamities."[10] The other important partition novel is Chaman Nahal's *Azadi*. The novel is built around the family of Lala Kanshi Ram, a grain merchant of Sialkot. Interwoven with it is the story of his son Arun, his aspirations and disappointments. The maturity and the balanced depiction of the carnage of partition gives Azadi a refreshing tone. The novel traces the origin of the trouble and moves to the final outrage in a tone devoid of sentimentalism and melodrama. Another important aspect of this novel is its experimentation with technique. The multiple narrator technique, used here for the first time, is a novel attempt in Indian-English fiction.

After independence came a process of reconstruction and rebuilding the nation. With the country striking a positive note in both domestic and international affairs, the period between the Fifties and Sixties was a productive period especially for literature. The independence movement as a motive force of the Indian English novel is replaced by a search for newer themes, in keeping with the emerging sensibility and concerns of a re-defined nation. Consequently, many of the novels deal with the East-West encounter, which obviously is a result of the unacknowledged colonial hangover. The protagonists struggle to find a place between two cultures, one inherited and the other acquired through education and other influences. The theme, however, is not new to the Indian English novel; as early as in 1909, Sarat Kumar Ghose wrote a novel called *The Prince of Destiny* dealing with this inter-cultural theme. The theme is brought out through the predicament of the protagonist when he has to choose between an English girl and a native Indian princess. During the Gandhian era, this conflict was more on the social level. But in the novel of the Sixties and Seventies, the predicament is on a personal level, leading to a crisis of identity. This private search often constitutes a quest for a satisfactory attitude towards the West, and for a realistic image of the East that would at the same time be emotionally valid. To quote Meenakshi Mukherjee, "This search has taken varied and complex forms. At its lowest, it has often descended into sentimental chauvinism and neurotic rejection, at its highest it has attempted an integration of personality, a revaluation of all values."[11] The typical Indian philosophical ideal of renunciation is explored in many novels as an answer to the search. It is impossible to definitely categorise the novels since there is the inevitable overlapping of the themes in the novels. Several major novels were published during the period. To name a few—*The Serpent and the Rope, The Cat and Shakespeare, The Guide, The Man-Eater of Malgudi, The Silver Pilgrimage, Shadow from Ladakh, Cry, the Peacock, Voices in the City, Sunlight on a Broken Column, The Foreigner, The Coffer Dams, A Bend in the Ganges, Chronicles of Kedaram, Too Long in the West, The Dark Dancer, Storm in*

Chandigarh etc.

A small note on the representative novels would illuminate the theme. Attia Hossain's *Sunlight on a Broken Column*, cast in the autobiographical mould, deals with the heroine's quest for her personal destiny as a result of the impact of the West on her. The West in this novel appears explicitly in terms of ideas rather than of persons. The resolution to her predicament is achieved through marriage. The conflict between the two cultures of East and West is nowhere so obviously spelled out as in Nayanatara Sahgal's first novel *A Time to be Happy*. The protagonist Sanad Shivpal's social background is the cause for his feeling of alienation and rootlessness. His predicament is once again solved when he marries the unsophisticated, non-westernised daughter of a college lecturer. In Balachandra Rajan's *The Dark Dancer*, the protagonist Krishnan's alienation is due to the conflict between the western influence and the native reality. The resolution of Krishnan's East-West dilemma hinges on his choice between Cynthia and Kamala who are representative symbols of the two cultures. Ultimately he resolves his predicament by embracing the traditional ideals of this country symbolised through Kamala.

The East-West theme moves into a different realm and assumes a depth and meaning not achieved in Indian English fiction with Raja Rao's *The Serpent and the Rope*. The novel is deeply philosophical in tone and metaphysical in demeanour. The protagonist Ramaswamy's predicament is resolved when he realises that he needs a guru to sort out the serpent from the rope. The solution, however, is a personal one. Here we see the theme of renunciation coming into prominence. This theme of renunciation can be best illustrated through R.K. Narayan's *The Guide*. The novel traces the development of Raju the protagonist; the worldliest of men is transformed in the course of the narrative into a sanyasi. In Bhattacharya's *He Who Rides a Tiger*, a marked change can be noticed in the tone and tenor of these novels. The Sixties' novel reflects a recognizable change in national sensibility, expression and literary form. As against the novel of the Thirties which shows concern with national or social problems, the novel of the Sixties has a distinctly private tone.

Commenting on the latter, Meenakshi Mukherjee points out that it is "introspective and the individual's quest for a personal meaning is its main theme."[12]

Compared to the Sixties there was no great spurt of activity in the Seventies. But still some significant novels were produced—Chaman Nahal's *Azadi* and *The English Queens*, Arun Joshi's *The Apprentice, The Strange Case of Billy Biswas*, Rama Mehta's *Inside the Haveli*, Anita Desai's *Bye-Bye, Blackbird*. The East-West conflict, the search for identity and the theme of renunciation continue. It becomes evident that an inevitable overlapping of themes takes place in these novels, thus making it difficult to deduce it to one fixed theme. In all these novels one notices that retreat is presented as a possible solution to the dilemmas of human life; this can be seen most prominently in Arun Joshi's *The Strange Case of Billy Biswas*. One comes to the conclusion that the novel of the Sixties and the Seventies operates within a limited range and affords easy solutions. The reasons for this reduced output in the Seventies are not too hard to see. Historically and politically, the Nineteen Seventies were one of the most turbulent decades in Indian history. The general decline on all fronts, the debilitating wars with Pakistan and finally the Emergency declared in 1975, put a severe check on national progress. The declaration of the Emergency dealt a deathblow to the Indian sensibility.

This taste of totalitarianism for a short time awoke the casual Indian from his slumber and lethargy. Having come so perilously close to losing his freedom, the Indian realised that from now on he had to play an important role in the making of history. As Viney Kirpal puts it, "The sudden realization of the reality of history in which the individual has an important role to play is reflected in the novel of the 1980s."[13] Thus the attempt by the individual to take an active role in the making of history is the important theme of the novel of the Eighties. The quest for identity is now against the background of a larger world; cosmopolitanism is the new reality. The new protagonist belongs everywhere; he is a cultural traveller and has the ability to merge into all cultures, coming to terms with the broadening horizons of modern experience. The novel of the Eighties exemplifies this theme. At this stage it would be worthwhile to recapitulate the tremendous contribution of the big three before elaborating on the novel of the Eighties. Mulk Raj Anand's explosive style of writing clearly left an indelible mark on the consciousness of a nation perpetrating atrocities on the less fortunate in the name of caste and religion. Starting with *Kanthapura* which dealt with the freedom movement, Raja Rao moves on to show his metaphysical concerns in *The Serpent and the Rope* and *The Cat and Shakespeare.* The range of his contribution to the Indian English novel can be summed up in his own words:

> Starting from the humanitarian and romantic aspect of man in *Kanthapura* and *The Cow and the Barricades*—both deeply influenced by Mahatma Gandhi's philosophy of non-violence, I soon came to the metaphysical novel, *The Serpent and the Rope* and *The Cat and Shakespeare* based on the vedantic conception of illusion and reality. My main interest increasingly is in showing the complexity of the human condition, and in showing the symbolic construct of one human expression. All words are hierarchic symbols, almost mathematical in precision, on and of the unknown.[14]

R.K. Narayan's contribution to the Indian English novel has been exemplary. Starting with *Swami and Friends*, his first novel published in 1938, to *The Painter of Signs* in 1993, he has captured the Indian imagination for well over seven decades. By his choice of themes and a unique style of presentation, he has carved a niche for himself in the crowded literary scene. His protagonists are all ordinary middle class people and the family constitutes the hub of his preoccupations. Commenting on the thematic concerns of Narayan's novels, William Walsh says, "The family, indeed, is the immediate context in which the novelist's sensibility operates, and his novels are remarkable for the subtlety with which family relationships are treated."[15] Thus in all his novels, *The English Teacher, The Bachelor of Arts, Waiting for the Mahatma* and *The Painter of Signs*, Narayan explores a variety of relationships within the family. Commenting on the plots of his novels, Walsh says, "The novels plot the rise of this intention onto awareness, its recognisation is a crisis of consciousness and then its resolution."[16]

Thus Mulk Raj Anand, with his concern for the destitute and the downtrodden, Raja Rao with his metaphysical preoccupations and Narayan with his depiction of socio-comic aspects of every-day life of ordinary people, put together a wide panorama of life. The recapitulation would be incomplete without the mention of G.V. Desani. When his novel *All About H. Hatterr* was published in 1948, it was considered a curious aberration. The irreverence with which the English language was used, the alteration in syntax and the manner in which it was presented made it a peculiar novel since it did not conform to predominant mode of his contemporaries, 'the big three.' It is written in what Anthony Burgess says, "whole language, in which philosophical terms, the colloquialisms of Calcutta and London, Shakespearean archaisms, whinings quack spiels, references to the Hindu pantheon, the jargon of Indian litigation, and irritability seethe together."[17] Salman Rushdie acknowledges the tremendous influence of G.V. Desani on his writing. Viney Kirpal commenting on the turbulent political scenario of the Nineteen Seventies says that "the 1970s were a gestation period for the shaping of the new Indian sensibility."[18] However, the whole body of Indian English novels really do not anticipate the novel of the Eighties. The content and the form of the novel of the Eighties are unique.

The sensation of the Eighties was the arrival on the Indian literary scene of Salman Rushdie's *Midnight's Children*. It not only shook the very foundations of the Indian English novel but also took the literary world by storm. Makarand Paranjape sums up accurately the impact of the novel: "This momentous book really jolted the very foundation of the Indian English novel. Its energy, self-indulgence, irresponsibility, disorder and cockiness really shocked the daylight out of the staid form of the Indian English novel."[19]

The daring innovation in terms of both theme and technique in *Midnight's Children* set the tone for the new novel of the

Eighties. And since then, there has been a steady output of novels, each being accorded critical acclaim. The novel of the Eighties recognises the plural nature of society and the importance of national integration. It thus reflects the reality of the mixed Indian tradition. The thrust in the new novel is on synthesis, an awareness of compelling plurality. The scope of these novels is trans-national and trans-continental. The East-West conflict projected in the novel of the Sixties is now a thing of the past. Now cultures mingle, as is evident when characters of different nationalities interact with ease. As a result the whole world is projected as one big home. The new individual is more cosmopolitan and deregionalised than in the novel of the Sixties and Seventies. Some of the important novels of the Eighties are *Midnight's Children, Rich like Us, Plans for Departure, Baumgartner's Bombay, Shame, The Circle of Reason, The Bubble, Sunrise in Fiji, The Shadow Lines.* These novelists with their choice of themes and techniques share the vision and objectives of other postcolonial writers. These postcolonial writers do exactly what *Times International* terms as their mission "to bring energy and outsider's freshness into the closed and almost airless rooms of English Literature."[20] In a lighter vein, the magazine remarks: "For centuries Britons set up their institutions in the wilds and brought their culture to the world; now the world is bringing back the wilds to British institutions."[21]

The three authors studied in this book occupy a pre-eminent place among the postcolonial novelists of the Eighties. Commencing their writing career in this momentous decade, they constitute a distinct group which exemplifies the essence of the novel of the Eighties. A study of their novels would thus provide an invaluable insight into the startlingly new developments in the Indian English novel.

That the most unsuspected arrival of Salman Rushdie's *Midnight's Children* on the literary scene in the year 1981 changed the very contours of the Indian English novel has already been mentioned. The impact of the novel on them can be best understood in the assessment of Klaus Borner, "It was something like a Copernican turning-point in the history of literature and ideas."[22] Panoramic in its scope, the narrative moves geographically through three nations and chronologically through six decades of the turbulent socio-political phase of the sub-continent. Though the novel teems with a vast array of characters, the protagonist Saleem Sinai's centrality is never in doubt. The course of his quest for identity is used as a means of drawing in the entire history of the sub-continent in its most significant phase. Rushdie puts into *Midnight's Children* virtually all of twentieth century Indian history, starting from the Jallianwalla Bagh and making its way through the Quit India movement, the Cabinet Mission, the role of the Muslim League in the partition, reorganization of Indian states, language riots, the Indo-China war, theft of the Prophet's hair from the Hazratbal mosque in Kashmir, the wars with Pakistan, the liberation of Bangladesh and finally the Emergency. Rushdie, by a marvellous stroke of ingenuity, weaves the historical with the life of some members of the protagonist's family. It is this aspect that elevates the novel from being a limited personal narrative into the realms of historical and political fiction. In a significant depiction of the close intertwining of history, politics and the individual, the development of the protagonist is seen running parallel to the growth of the nation.

Divided into three parts, the first part of *Midnight's Children* traces the family roots in Kashmir, its move to Bombay via Amritsar, Agra and Delhi and ends with Saleem Sinai's birth; the second deals with the family's sojourn in Bombay, followed by a shift to Pakistan and ends with the 1965 Indo-Pakistan war; the third covers the carnage in East-Pakistan and the creation of Bangladesh and ends with the Emergency and its aftermath. Chronologically it can also be divided into three sections, indicating the importance of the historical factor in the narrative—pre-Independence, Partition and post-Independence.

The narrative begins in Kashmir in the year 1915, much before the birth of Saleem Sinai. This section depicts the circumstances under which Dr. Aadam Aziz moves from Kashmir to Amritsar and how he is drawn into the maelstrom of the freedom movement. At the same time, incidents and characters are used to indicate the forces which will lead to the ultimate horror of partition. But they also suggest those positive elements which will be the saving grace in that traumatic period. The Jallianwallah Bagh massacre intensifies Aadam Aziz's sense of nationalism as it did with millions of Indians at that time. At the time when Muslim fundamentalist forces were raising their sinister heads aggravating communal tensions by vociferously demanding partition, characters like Mian Abdullah hold out a ray of hope through their broader vision of a brotherhood transcending communal barriers. Aadam Aziz's involvement in the freedom struggle is unassuming but sincere and committed. With the dramatic entry of Saleem Sinai, the family connection with the history of the nation takes a more direct and flamboyant turn. He is handcuffed to history by virtue of being born at the same momentous hour of the nation's independence. Hailed as the Mubarak by the soothsayers, his birth acknowledged by the Prime Minister himself, Saleem feels that he has a special destiny. With the special powers of telepathy he possesses, Saleem envisages a decisive role for himself in guiding the history of the new nation. His family members rather rudely ground his presumptions of being a Messiah. This paradoxically comes as a blessing as he now retreats to the privacy of an old clock tower from where he convenes the midnight children's conference, comprising other children also born during the midnight hour and possessing extraordinary powers like himself. Saleem desires to harness their powers to guide the destiny of the nation. Dissensions by way of selfish interests and language bias subvert the lofty ideals, as a result of which Saleem's vision suffers a severe setback. The midnight's child who gives Saleem the most trouble is Shiva, his alter ego, the child exchanged during birth by Mary Pereira. During the course of his childhood, Saleem, whose face resembles the map of India, suffers many mutilations, symbolic of the fractured growth of the infant nation. Not being able to take an active role in guiding the history of the nation, doubts begin to creep into his mind leading to a crisis of identity. Constant shifting of locations also adds to this crisis. His family's sojourn in Pakistan is the most miserable period for Saleem as he is forced to abstain from his midnight children's conference and also becomes an innocent participant in the bizarre politics of Pakistan. Saleem's joy on returning to Bombay is short-lived, as a sinus operation completely deprives him of all contact with the midnight children. He is however compensated for this loss by a superior sense of smell, which at a later stage gives him the bizarre identity of the buddha.

The shifting of the family permanently to Pakistan a few years later is the beginning of the second stage of Saleem's quest for identity. But disappointments on both the personal and social fronts aggravate the crisis. To make matters worse, his central place in the scheme of all things in which he took a lot of pride is usurped by his sister Jamila Singer, who by her melodious voice becomes the darling of the nation. A forlorn and despondent Saleem takes to wandering. The war over Kashmir between India and Pakistan, for which he takes the responsibility, comes to his rescue. The war annihilates all his family members, and the silver spittoon, the family heirloom, mercifully drains him of all memory. The crisis of identity now reaches a state of total negation. Realising his potential as a sniffer, the Pakistan army now puts him to use by assigning him the task of a sniffer dog to sniff out insurgents in East Pakistan. It is at this time that his companions in his group give him the identity of the buddha due to his appearance and enigmatic character. The group's participation in the assault on human dignity finds its nemesis in the Sundarbans. Saleem gets back his memory there under unusual circumstances. On emerging from the Sundarbans, the group is shocked to see the carnage caused by war.

Saleem returns to India in the magic basket of Parvati, another midnight child. In Delhi now, in the magicians' ghetto, Saleem embarks on his search for an identity, now on his own terms. His attempts to enlist the help of his uncle Mustapha not only fail but the association also becomes responsible for his downfall in the end. Saleem's last attempt in his search is through his association with Picture Singh, the snake charmer. It is through Picture Singh that Saleem is reunited with his surrogate mother Mary Pereira, now the owner of the highly successful Braganza pickle factory in Bombay. Thus the novel makes a full circle. But before this reunion, Saleem suffers one last and the most devastating mutilation at the hands of the "widow." The emergency declared by the widow proves disastrous for the midnight children, as she perceives them to be a threat to her political authority. His alter ego once again appears in the narrative for the last time. He has played the role of Shiva of myth. His union with Parvati is brilliantly brought out. In the end Saleem pins all his hopes on his son Aadam Sinai, Emergency's child, who really is the son of Shiva and Parvati. Saleem is confident that the new generation would be stronger and emerge victorious in the quest. By attempting to create history, Saleem has become the beacon light for future generations.

In his next novel *Shame* published in 1983, Rushdie focusses on a fictitious country Peccavistan, which however is a thin disguise for Pakistan. It is a narrative replete with symbolism, fantasy and political overtones and yet filled with human drama.

The political and social repression unleashed by an authoritarian state is woven into the protagonist Omar Khayyam Shakil's search for his own personal identity in such an environment. In the course of his search for identity, the protagonist moves through three distinct phases. The first phase deals with Omar Khayyam Shakil suffering a crisis of identity in Nishapur, a mansion which is the very embodiment of 'shamelessness,' one of the recurrent themes in the novel. Born under mysterious circumstances, Omar Khayyam's crisis commences right from the time of his birth. The first twelve years of his life are spent in the unnatural environs of Nishapur closeted with his three embittered mothers who teach him that shamelessness is a virtue. A voracious reader, Omar Khayyam masters the art of hypnosis even as a young boy. This knowledge of hypnosis comes in handy for him during the most crucial stage of his life later on. In the second phase of his development, Omar Khayyam Shakil attempts to break free from the stifling unhealthy environment of Nishapur. His entry into the outside world for the first time is replete with drama. His schooldays do not pass innocuously as the lesson of shamelessness is too deeply instilled in him. His first victim of hypnosis is his hapless classmate Farah Zoraster.

Quite oblivious to her suffering, he leaves Q to study medicine in Karachi.

On the professional front he gains a high reputation as a doctor, but on the personal front, he continues to lead a life of abject shamelessness. Omar Khayyam Shakil's close associate in his misdemeanours is Isky Harappa, soon to play a major role in the political scenario of the country. The personal and the political strands of the story are thus cleverly integrated. Isky Harappa's political ambitions lead him to summarily discard Omar Khayyam Shakil who now latches on to Raza Hyder, the emerging star on the political scene. Through his association with Raza Hyder, he comes into contact with his mentally retarded daughter Sufiya Zenobia, the symbol of shame in the novel. The association originally commencing on a professional note, he eventually marries her, thus completing the symbolic union of shame and shamelessness in the novel. Sufiya is simultaneously symbolic of the effects of repression on the human psyche and the indication of the ultimate destruction of such forces. The backlash to the social and political outrage heaped on a people by successive political leaders is symbolically represented by Sufiya's violence. Towards the end she becomes a mythic creature unleashing terrifying violence, obviously representing the nation's outrage. The final stage in Omar Khayyam Shakil's quest for identity involves a process of correction. In his affection and sincere concern for Sufiya, he not only discards his unsavoury identity but also forges a more humane consciousness. Simultaneously the narrative takes us through the political nemesis of both Isky Harappa and Raza Hyder. Symbolically, the narrative concludes with the destruction of Nishapur, the mansion of shamelessness, by Sufiya, the living symbol of the shame of repression.

Another significant novel *The Circle of Reason* published in 1986, displays like *Midnight's Children* the cosmopolitanism which is characteristic of the novel of the Eighties. This novel of Amitav Ghosh deals with the picaresque adventures of the young protagonist Alu, who in his search for identity, moves from rural Bengal to the mythical Eastern 'boom' city of al-

Ghazira and finally to El-Oued, a desert town in Algeria. The three sections of the novel constitute the three stages of the protagonist's search for identity taking place in three different countries.

In the long opening section, the story unfolds in a small village Lalpukur near Calcutta, where the young orphaned protagonist arrives. The first stage in his search for identity in India depicts the protagonist as a mere observer of passions of various kinds. Alu observes his schoolteacher uncle, Balaram Bose's passion for phrenology, Reason and Pasteur. These passions manifest themselves in various ways. His obsession with phrenology is the beginning of an acrimonious relationship with Bhudeb Roy, the ambitious and unscrupulous local politician cum headmaster. Balaram Bose's passion for Reason leads him to establish the Pasteur School of Reason, whose rise and fall is replete with drama. His obsession with cleanliness leads him to the indiscriminate and inhuman use of carbolic acid in the village. This obsession brings him into direct confrontation with Bhudeb Roy. Alu is also an observer of Bhudeb Roy's passion for power and greed for money. At his instigation, Balaram Bose's house is raided by the police on two counts of harbouring terrorists and abetting the elopement of his wife Parboti Debi with Shombu Debnath, the enigmatic local weaver, to whom Alu is apprenticed. The innocent boy is caught in the crossfire of two men trying to destroy one another. In the climax of the Lalpukur section, Balaram Bose is blown to smithereens in a bizarre confrontation with Bhudeb Roy and the police, the inevitable outcome of his blind passions. Alu is saved by a miraculous quirk of fate, but now branded an extremist, is forced to flee the village, shadowed by the policeman Jyoti Das.

On the run now, Alu first reaches Calcutta and then moves to the south, always just managing to elude the police and Jyoti Das, till he finally reaches Mahe, the southern most part of India's west coast. Alu, still trying to evade the reach of the police, decides to set sail over the Indian Ocean to al-Ghazira.

In distant al-Ghazira Alu's search continues. This section teems with a variety of characters like Nuri, the one-eyed egg seller, Jeevavbhai Patel, the ruined business man, Professor Samuel, the eccentric accountant, Karthamma, Kulfi, who plays an important role towards the end and, the most fascinating of all, Zindi, the big-hearted madam who keeps open house and befriends Alu on the boat journey to al-Ghazira.

However the focus among the many stories and incidents continues to be on Alu's search for identity. The episode in which Alu lies buried under the rubble of 'The Star' constitutes the most momentous experience of this phase of his search. It marks a definite movement from being a mere observer to becoming a more active participant in his own story. Miraculously rescued from the rubble, he emerges for the first time with his own definite views on the necessity of purging the world of the evils of money. His quixotic scheme to destroy this evil backfires, leading this time to a self-created disaster. Alu's life reaches a state of stasis, symbolized by his atrophied thumbs. Rescued by Zindi, he moves along with Kulfi and the child Boss to El-Oued to play out the last stage of his search for identity.

In El-Oued, Mrs. Verma, an Indian doctor, who gives the final turn to Alu's search, befriends the fugitive party. Brisk and no-nonsensical, she is still filled with a human warmth and concern. The manner, in which she handles the tragic death of Kulfi, and overcoming all hurdles, gives the body a dignified and ceremonial burial, turns out to be the most significant influence on Alu. Ironically he picks up the most important values of life from a tragic situation—the idea that for a sane and balanced life, passion should be moderated by genuine human concern. This idea could not have been better demonstrated through the act of consigning Balaram Bose's book *Life of Pasteur* to the flames. The circle is complete.

The new cosmopolitan experience seen in *The Circle of Reason* is explored in greater depth in Amitav Ghosh's second novel *The Shadow Lines* published in 1988. The cosmopolitanism this time moves beyond being a mere geographical shift of location in the narrative to a broader examination of the inter-action of cultures, and the individual's attempt to find a place in this interaction.

The protagonist's search for identity takes place through his interaction with a cluster of significant characters who expose him to their own individual perceptions of living in the modern world. The unnamed protagonist is positioned amidst the cross-currents of these influences from which he ultimately manages to mould his individual consciousness.

The first section of the novel traces vividly the unnamed protagonist's childhood experiences. As a child, he is a great admirer of his strict disciplinarian grandmother. He gets his first lesson in the meaning of nationalism by the stories she relates to him of her student days in Dhaka during the freedom struggle. The other character who grows on his consciousness is his enigmatic uncle Tridib. He captures the young boy's imagination by his encyclopaedic knowledge and especially by the way he instructs him to use his imagination. Tridib opens out a new and broader world to the young protagonist, and perhaps gives him his first lesson in a cosmopolitanism which is of mental attitude rather than physical location.

The contrast between these two aspects of cosmopolitanism is embodied in the character of his cousin Ila. By virtue of her father being in the diplomatic service, Ila has travelled extensively, but her lack of imagination has severely checked her perceptions of other nations and their cultures. The protagonist is exactly the opposite of Ila, in the sense that he has seen much without having travelled at all, whereas Ila in spite of having travelled much, has seen nothing at all. The concept of cosmopolitanism is extended further when the protagonist moves to London, and with the introduction of Nick and May Price, into the narrative. Ila's ill-fated fascination for Nick Price, a man with a dubious reputation, is used to bring out the lacunae in her brand of cosmopolitanism. Her blind fascination for a western way of life leads her into a disastrous marriage with Nick Price, a marriage she regards as an entry into the apparently liberated western society. In her desperate pre-occupation with attaining a cosmopolitan identity, she is dangerously detached from her cultural roots. The protagonist perceives that everything about her has a ring of falsehood about it. As a contrast to Ila, May Price, with her genuine commitment to social work and an intense human concern embodies an authentic cosmopolitan consciousness. The search for identity takes its final form when the narrative shifts to Bangladesh. As in *The Circle of Reason* it is a tragic situation which delivers the message. Tridib dies a gory death at the hands of a frenzied communal mob on the streets of Dhaka thus exploding the myth of the "shadow line" supposed to be separating nations. In other words Tridib becomes a victim of parochial sentiments. With Tridib's death, an element of irrational and frenzied emotion seeps into Tha'mma's passionate nationalism. The protagonist becomes aware of the shortcomings of such a consciousness in the context of a larger world.

In the course of his search for identity, the protagonist realises the necessity of striking a rational balance between indiscriminate cosmopolitanism and blind irrational nationalism. The ability to imaginatively identify with other cultures while retaining one's native cultural roots becomes necessary in the broadening horizons of the modern world.

The third important novelist of the Eighties decade Upamanyu Chatterjee published his maiden novel *English, August: An Indian Story* in 1988, which deals with the contemporary youth's search for identity. Agastaya Sen the young I.A.S. officer's sense of dislocation when suddenly transplanted from his megalopolitan background to the realities of life in a small backward town Madna is emblematic of the predicament of young Indians with similar backgrounds. Their cosmopolitan upbringing is a powerful alienating force, leading to a disturbing sense of rootlessness, disillusionment and disaffection. The narrative takes the protagonist through different stages in his attempt to come to terms with the new environment. In the course of his quest, he moves from a debilitating sense of alienation to an urge towards escapism and finally finds his own solution through a positive involvement in the compelling realities of life in this country.

Agastaya's arrival in the hot, dusty, unglamorous town of Madna triggers off an acute sense of dislocation. He is jolted out of the placid, complacent attitude he had so carefully cultivated.

Adding to his woes is his inability to adjust to the mindless functioning of a pompous bureaucratic set-up. In Madna, he encounters a variety of people who hold out possible ways of overcoming his sense of dissatisfaction and alienation. Finding all these unacceptable, he takes recourse to escapism and retreats into an enclosed world of his own. As a result he is compelled to lead three lives in Madna to keep up his social and official pretences. This juggling with three lives confounds him further, leading to an acute sense of alienation.

After a certain stage, Agastaya's inability to cope with the pressure reaches a state of mental stasis. He feels that a return to his megalopolitan roots would show the way out of his disturbing predicament. Contrary to those expectations, he finds himself in further confusion when he discovers his friends in Delhi suffering from a similar rootlessness. Back in Madna, his mind opens out to positive influences. His association with Govind Sathe, a journalist who introduces him to the *Bhagvad Gita*, leads him to a hitherto unattempted search for solutions. John Avery's determined and single-minded devotion to a dream, Baba Ramanna's humanitarian work for the rehabilitation of leprosy patients, the devoted work of the Naxalites to create awareness among the exploited tribals and the Fisher King's determination to divine a meaning in life, are eye-opening influences. Agastaya's chance for positive action comes when he takes constructive steps to alleviate the acute water shortage in a remote tribal village. Agastaya realises that the solution to rootlessness does not lie in negativism or escapism but in positive human concern and constructive action. Having disinvested himself of his former attitude of disconcern and detachment, Agastaya leaves Madna a changed man, a man with a new vision.

Thus a historical survey of the Indian English novel shows that the configuration of the novel has changed from time to time and found expression according to the perception of the writer. The varieties of themes which have been dealt with have been discussed in the earlier part of the chapter. The entire body of literature surveyed, though significant, does not however fully anticipate either in theme or technique the overwhelming originality of *Midnight's Children*. *Midnight's Children* gave the gamut of the Indian English novel a thorough overhaul. Its theme and technique set a revolutionary trend bringing the hitherto insular Indian English novel in tune with developments in post-colonial literatures all over the world. Salman Rushdie's contemporaries Amitav Ghosh and Upamanyu Chatterjee have continued the trend, each focussing on certain selected aspects. These new writers have carved a niche for themselves in the sphere of post-colonial literatures. Like their fellow writers all over the world, they have moved into a trans-cultural ethos. As Pico Iyer succinctly comments: "They are something different. For one thing they are the products not so much as of a colonial division as of the international culture that has grown up, and they are addressing an audience as mixed up and eclectic and uprooted as themselves. They are the creators and creations of a new post-imperial order. English is the lingua franca; just about everywhere is a suburb of the same international culture."[23]

This new sensibility and the new ethos find comprehensive expression in the novel of the Eighties. This study is an attempt to explore the manner in which the authors individually and as a group give expression to these altered perceptions. This change in perceptions has, thematically, been viewed through two particular aspects—the radically different view of the interaction between history, politics and the individual and the new dimensions given to the traditional issue of the search for identity. In terms of technique, the book explores the manner in which the Indian English novel has opened out under the influence of post-colonial techniques without detaching it from its traditional moorings. It is hoped that this study will provide significant insights into this highly challenging field.

NOTES

1. Krishna Kripalani, *Indian Literature: A Panoramic Glimpse* (Bombay: Nirmal Sadanand, 1969), p. 45.
2. K.R. Srinivasa Iyengar, *Indian Writing in English* (New Delhi:

Sterling, 1990), p. 315.

3. Meenakshi Mukherjee, *The Twice-Born Fiction* (New Delhi: Arnold Heinemann, 1971), p. 34.
4. William Walsh, *Indian Literature in English* (Harlow: Longman, 1990), p. 62.
5. M.K. Naik, *Gandhi in Literature* (Mysore: University of Mysore 1971), p. 57.
6. Iyengar, p. 324.
7. C.D. Narasimhaiah, "*Kanthapura*: An Analysis," *Critical Essays on Indian Writing in English*, ed. M.K. Naik (Dharwar: Karnatak University, 1968), p. 48.
8. Mukherjee, pp. 199-200.
9. Iyengar, p. 319.
10. Walsh, p. 99.
11. Mukherjee, p. 77.
12. Mukherjee, p. 198.
13. Viney Kirpal, *The New Indian Novel in English* (New Delhi: Allied, 1990), p. xxi.
14. Raja Rao, *Contemporary Novelists*, ed. James Vinson (London and Chicago, 1972), p. 1042.
15. Walsh, p. 74.
16. Walsh, p. 75.
17. Anthony Burgess, Introduction, *All About H. Hatterr*, by G.V. Desani (London: The Bodley Head, 1970), p. 10.
18. Viney Kirpal, p. xx.
19. Makarand R. Paranjape, "Inside and Outside the Whale: Politics in the New Indian Novel," *New Indian Novel in English*, ed. Viney Kirpal, p. 220.
20. Pico Iyer, "The Empire Writes Back," *Time International*, 8 Feb. 1993, p. 49.
21. Iyer, p. 51.
22. Klaus Borner, "The Reception of *Midnight's Children* in West Germany," *The Novels of Salman Rushdie*, ed. G.R. Taneja and R.K. Dhawan (New Delhi: Indian Society for Commonwealth Studies, 1992), p. 12.
23. Iyer, p. 49.

History, Politics and the Individual

History and politics have always been a predominant preoccupation of the Indian-English novelist. This compulsive obsession was perhaps inevitable since the genre developed concurrently with the climactic phase of colonial rule, the stirrings of nationalist sentiment and its full flowering in the final stages of the freedom movement. The Indian English novel developed at a time when the consciousness of being a part of history was a national phenomenon. The intense emotional stirring of a people united in the effort to break free from the shackles of foreign rule made individuals unusually conscious of being a part of a momentous historical movement. This consciousness is exemplified in the novels of Mulk Raj Anand, Raja Rao, Manohar Malgonkar with R.K. Narayan providing glimpses; it also finds expression in the later novels of Khushwant Singh, Chaman Nahal and Attia Hossain.

Therefore the theme of History, Politics and the Individual might not appear as particular to the novel of the Eighties. However, the difference of treatment—a shift in the focus, a new array of techniques through which the theme is expressed—gives it an indisputable novelty. History and politics dominated the proceedings in the earlier novels but with the individual relegated to the periphery. The individual gets lost in the movement as can be seen in Raja Rao's *Kanthapura* or R.K. Narayan's *Waiting for the Mahatma* or Manohar Malgonkar's *A Bend in the Ganges*. The novels on partition, *Train to Pakistan* and *Azadi* present the individuals as helpless victims of historical forces. The image of history projected in these novels is that of a Juggernaut rolling impassively over all that comes within its purview. In the novel of the Eighties, the hitherto peripheral individual is thrust into the centre-stage, no longer linked to history as a passive victim but projected as himself an agent of history. Rushdie, in whose novels this perspective is present in the most striking manner, is a self-consciously theoretical novelist who has propounded his own theory of history. He regards individuals as being linked to history in several ways as he explains in *Midnight's Children*.[1]

> I was linked to history both literally and metaphorically, both actively and passively, modes of connection composed of dualistically combined-configurations. . . . This is why hyphens are necessary: actively-literally, passively-metaphorically, actively-metaphorically and passively-literally, I was inextricably entwined with my world. By the combination of "active" and "literal" I mean, of course, all actions of mine which directly—literally—affected, or altered the course of, seminal historical events, for instance the manner in which I provided the language marchers with the battle cry. The union of "passive" and "metaphorical" encompasses all socio-political trends and events which, by existing, affected me metaphorically—for example, by reading between the lines of the episode entitled "The Fisherman's Pointing Finger," you will perceive the unavoidable connection between the infant state's attempts at rushing towards full-sized adulthood and my own early, explosive efforts at growth. . . . Next, "passive" and "literal," when hyphenated, cover all moments at which national events had a direct bearing upon the lives of myself and my family—under this heading you should file the freezing of my father's assets, and also the explosion at Walkeshwar Reservoir, which unleashed the cat invasion. And finally there is the "mode" of the "active-metaphorical," which groups together the occasions on which things done by me or to me were mirrored in the macrocosm of public affairs, and my private existence was shown to be symbolically at one with history. The mutilation of my middle finger was a case in point, because when I was detached from my fingertip and blood (neither Alpha nor Omega) rushed out in fountains, a

> similar thing happened to history, and all sorts of every-whichthing began pouring out all over us.

History then is linked to the individual in three ways. Raghavendra Rao succinctly sums up the lengthy passage, as "history bearing, history suffering and history creating."[2] In "On the Uses and Disadvantage of History for Life," Nietzsche discusses the three modes of historical consciousness—"the unhistorical," which comprises the power of "forgetting," of limiting one's horizon, the historical, which is what we understand by conventional history—the paralysing "burden of history," finally the super-historical—a sense that allows for a greater cultural view.[3] The last mode of history creating as expounded by Rushdie is similar to Nietzsche's super-historical mode. Commenting on this last mode, David W. Price says, "Only he who is oppressed . . . and wants to throw off this burden at any cost, has the need for critical history."[4]

While the earlier novels focussed on individuals as history bearing and history suffering, the novels of the Eighties project the history-creating individual. The myth of history as Juggernaut is diffused. Being a product of the post-Independence generation, the novel of the Eighties primarily focuses on the post-Independence scenario and projects the individual in a hitherto unexplored role as history creating. The glimpses of pre-Independence and Partition years expose the limitations of the earlier perspective. This chapter has been divided into three sections dealing with the pre-Independence, Partition and post-Independence eras respectively, in order to focus on the new perceptions of the link between history and the individual.

Historical forces have a tremendous effect on almost all things in the world today. To quote Walter Allen:

> In the literature of an age, its conflicts, tendencies, obsessions are uncovered and made manifest to a degree which is continually astonishing; good writers are, so to speak, mediumistic to the deeper stirrings of life of their time while they are still unknown to, or at any rate unsuspected

> by, the public, politicians and current received opinion . . . contemporary novels are the mirror of the age, but a very special kind of mirror that reflects not merely the external features of the age but also its inner face, its nervous system, coursing of its blood and the unconscious promptings and conflicts which sway it.[5]

The novels of Salman Rushdie, Amitav Ghosh and Upamanyu Chatterjee are mirrors of this kind, establishing a dynamic interaction between the individual and the multifarious forces of history. Uma Parameswaran emphasizes this aspect with particular reference to Rushdie: "What Rushdie has done in *Midnight's Children*, is to recognize and demonstrate that the Indian situation is the perfect metaphor for characteristically twentieth-century questions about history, language, social and political fragmentation and creativity. Whereas Narayan's view in *Waiting for the Mahatma* or Singh's view in *Train to Pakistan*, for example is microcosmic, Rushdie's view in *Midnight's Children* is certainly macrocosmic. India, because of its size and complexity, and the fecundity of its myth and cult is the ideal metaphor for the plight of the individual and history."[6]

Constantly ruminating, grappling with the current complex issues, and trying to come to terms with the present, the novel of the Eighties still finds it imperative to constantly go back to the past. Amitav Ghosh, Salman Rushdie and Upamanyu Chatterjee intersperse their narratives with incidents from the pre-Independence struggle and the Partition holocaust. The new techniques in these novels do not present incidents and events of history in chronological order. Current events bring to focus events of the past. So artistically is the new and old synthesized that events of the past come alive, making it a living experience. In another significant way, the novels of the Eighties present a radically different perception of history. History is no more the biographies of kings and queens but finds an important place for the common man as an active participant in the making of history. Salman Rushdie is deeply concerned with the politics of the sub-continent.

In an interview given to Gordon Wise, Salman Rushdie calls himself "a fairly political animal." In the course of the interview, he claims that his novels "*Midnight's Children* and *Shame* are novels on historical themes."[7]

His presentation of politics and history is innovative. The fusing of these two aspects with the life of the individual has been done with dexterity and imaginative power. Thus he fulfills, what he had said earlier about the purpose of writing *Midnight's Children*, "to relate private lives to public events and to explore the limits of individuality in a country as populous and culturally variegated as India."[8] *Shame* attempts a similar exploration against the politico-historical scenario of Pakistan. These novels try to highlight complex networks of transcultural relationship between the individual and historical forces. "It seems to me," Rushdie remarks, "that everything in both books has had to do with politics and with the relationship of the individuals and history."[9] Rushdie's belief that one cannot separate history and the individual as "they interpenetrate and that is how the writer needs to examine them, the one in the context of the other"[10] is best exemplified in Saleem Sinai's flamboyant claim that he is "handcuffed to history." (3) The narrator protagonist feels that "his destiny is indissolubly chained to those of my [his] country." (3) Niel Ten Kortenaar comments, "Salman Rushdie's *Midnight's Children* is commonly read as a national allegory giving imaginative form to India and its history."[11]

This aspect can be seen when Rushdie puts into *Midnight's Children* virtually all of twentieth century history—the Jallianwala Bagh incident, Quit India movement, the Cabinet Mission, the Muslim League and its role in the partitioning of the country, riots and bloodshed subsequent to Independence, the Five-Year Plans, re-organisation of Indian states, language riots, the war with China, the theft of the sacred relic from the Hazratbal mosque in Kashmir, the wars with Pakistan, the liberation of Bangladesh and finally the emergency. There are also other events which show the typical Indian co-existence of discordant elements—religious fanaticism juxtaposed with secular ideals.

Incidents from pre-Independence clearly focus on the mammoth human struggle for freedom. The will to be free and unbounded is the central point in all the novels. The patriotic fervour, the tireless endeavour, the unflagging human spirit and the inner strength are highlighted and are the point of focus. The novels capture the variety and range of the individual's involvement in the nationalist movement. Some of them in the fight for freedom chose the militant path and some others the path of non-violence. What was common was the fire of freedom raging relentlessly in everyone's heart. In the course of depicting this struggle, the novels present individuals as being engulfed by the forces of history. Hence the individual is presented as history bearing.

The writers of the Eighties also show that the suffering did not end with the coming of freedom. The partition drama is depicted as a nightmarish experience with the individual in his role of history suffering, the victim of the inexorable forces of history. The new novel with its innovativeness enables the post-Independence generation to imaginatively re-live that horrendous experience. The novels show that the post-Independence scenario is equally challenging. Today the word politics has acquired a variety of unpleasant meanings. The novelists show the titanic struggle of the individual in the post-Independence era against Herculean odds. His efforts to create a new positive history emphasize the idea of the individual as history creating.

The historico-political consciousness of Rushdie is blatantly on display. In Amitav Ghosh and Upamanyu Chatterjee, this consciousness is given a more muted expression. They deal with the inextricable link between history and the individual in less concentrated but equally meaningful manner.

Hence this chapter is divided into three sections namely pre-Independence—showing the individual as history bearing, Partition—showing the individual as history suffering and the post-Independence—showing the individual as history creating.

The demarcation may not be universally acceptable because of the inevitable overlapping of the categories. However it has been found convenient as a means of organizing this study to maintain a necessary focus on the new dynamic connection being established between history and the individual.

Pre-Independence: The Individual as History Bearing

Through an encapsulation of the experiences of the three generations of the Sinai family, the narrative of *Midnight's Children* moves through the pre-Independence, Partition and the post-Independence eras of contemporary Indian history. Saleem Sinai, the narrator protagonist, fuses public events with his personal life and that of his family. From Kashmir to Amritsar and from there to Agra and from Agra to Delhi, Saleem narrates the journey of his maternal grandparents Dr. Aadam Aziz and his wife Naseem. With the progress of the story of the journey, we see the progress of the Indian struggle for Independence from Jallianwala Bagh to the partition of India. Dr. Aadam Aziz passes through various situations, which are connected with every turn in the march of Indian history. Commenting on the role of Dr. Aadam Aziz, Neeraja Mattoo says: "Through Aziz's story we are introduced to one of the important themes in this study of India; the juxtaposition of the old and the new, the myth ridden fabulous past and its attendant narrowness and prejudice on the one hand and modernism which brings its own problems on the other."[12]

The actual connection between Dr. Aziz and history is set into motion when in Kashmir, old Tai, the shikara man, brings a summons to him to treat the blind landowner's daughter Naseem. The perforated sheet, through which Dr. Aziz gets partial glimpses of his future bride, is a symbolic anticipation of the fragmented history of India, which is to unfold. Dr. Aziz's relationship with his "sectioned" patient Naseem keeps pace with the developments of the First World War:

> Far away the Great War moved from crisis to crisis, while in the cobwebbed house Doctor Aziz was also engaged in a total war against his 'sectioned' patient's inexhaustible complaints. On the day the World War ended, Naseem developed the longed-for headache. Such historical co-incidences have littered and perhaps befouled my family's existence in the world. (23)

Dr. Aziz has his first brush with Indian history when he comes to Amritsar with his newly wed wife Naseem. He is quick to reject the Rowlatt Act banning political agitation. On April 7th, 1919, the strike called by Gandhi turns violent. Dr. Aziz plunges into the movement by treating the wounded. His sympathies are aroused. He realizes that there is some horrendous event waiting in the wings. A sardonic humour characteristic of Rushdie, his adeptness at fusing the grand and the trivial is evident when the premonition of the historical Jallianwala Bagh event is linked to the itching of Dr. Aziz's nose. On April 13th, 1919, Brigadier Dyer ordered the massacre of one thousand five hundred and sixteen unarmed people gathered at the Jallianwala Bagh. This incident seems to embody the helplessness of the common man caught in the whirlwind of history. Saleem Sinai, who is narrating this incident, does so by being scrupulously truthful and providing a factual report, as opposed to a partisan, nationalistic, religious or cultural viewpoint. He resorts to understatement rather than melodramatic rhetoric when he describes the shooting in Jallianwala Bagh by Brigadier General Dyer's men:

> Brigadier Dyer's fifty men put down their machine guns and went away. They have fired a total of one thousand six hundred and fifty rounds into the unarmed crowd. Of these, one thousand five hundred and sixteen have found their mark, killing or wounding some person. Good shooting, Dyer tells his men we have done a jolly good thing. (35)

Tariq Rehman aptly sums up General Dyer's actions when he says, "General Dyer's words bring out his inhumanity in particular and the whole phenomenon of colonial rule in general."[13] Rushdie's style of narration seems unemotional but it unleashes deeper emotions which could not have been evoked by melodrama.

On the day Dr. Aziz witnesses the Jallianwallah Bagh massacre, many new realizations dawn on him. The impact of the senseless massacre is not limited to the emotional. His association with Mian Abdullah transforms this into a desire for positive action. Mian Abdullah or 'the Humming bird' rose from the famous magicians' ghetto in Delhi to become "the hope—of India's hundred million Muslims." (40) Mian Abdullah was the founder of the free Islamic convocation, an organization to counteract the Muslim League's designs for a separate country for the Muslims. Under his tutelage, Dr. Aziz's identification with the secular ideals of India is complete. He tells the Rani of Coonch Naheen, "I started off as a Kashmiri and not much of a Muslim, then I got a bruise on the chest that turned me into an Indian, though not much of a Muslim but I'm all for Abdullah." (40) His secular outlook is evident when he dismisses the maulvi, his children's tutor. He tells his wife Naseem that the maulvi was "teaching them to hate. . . . Hindus, Buddhists, Jain and Sikh." (40) He refuses to let his children grow up hating others. With his association with Mian Ahdullah, Aziz's zest for freedom grows into an "optimism disease" which is sweeping through the hearts of all liberal Indians. With the gruesome death of Mian Abdullah at the hands of fanatic Muslim Leaguers, the idea of a united India is scuttled. The "optimism disease" comes to a premature and disillusioned end. Dr. Aziz is left in tears of grief. Nevertheless Aziz's brush and association with incidents of history had made him more determined, humane and secular in outlook; he "buried himself in his work, taking upon himself the nursing of the sick in the shanty towns by the railway tracks—rescuing them from quacks who injected them with pepper water, and thought that fried spiders could cure blindness." (56) He thus plunged into social work at the service of millions of poverty-stricken, exploited people. The connection between the individual and history is reiterated through passing references to other members of Dr. Aziz's family. The parallelism between the disintegration of the marriage of Mumtaz Aziz, his daughter and Nadir Khan and the atomic explosion in Japan during the Second World War is blatant in its artifice. After three years of marriage, a bomb is dropped on Mumtaz and Nadir Khan's relationship. Simultaneously, on a fateful day a weapon such as the world had never seen was being dropped on the 'yellow people' in Japan. In Agra, her sister Emerald unleashed a secret weapon of her own, the bandy-legged, short, flat headed Zulfikir, placing him on Nadir Khan's track. The latter disappears, bringing the unconsummated marriage to an explosive end.

Rushdie's linking of history, politics and the individual often seems forced and contrived. However, the sheer verve of the writing and the exuberance of his imagination entices the reader into "a willing suspension of disbelief."

Amitav Ghosh in his two novels, *The Shadow Lines*[14] and *The Circle of Reason*[15] provides interesting glimpses of various facets of the Nationalist movement. Militant nationalism, socialism, non-violence were all paths leading to the common goal of independence. However diverse the paths chosen, the individual ultimately gets submerged in the movement and is relegated to the state of being a mere bearer of history.

The Shadow Lines, written in 1988, also deals with political issues. As Novy Kapadia comments, "It is basically a memory novel which skilfully weaves together, personal lives and public events in three countries—India, England and Bangladesh."[16] Amitav Ghosh through his narrative technique that includes a subtle sense of humour and an awareness of contemporary politics that is similar to Salman Rushdie, brings out the connection between private turmoil and crisis with their public counterparts. Certain incidents from the united pre-Independence India are narrated in an explicitly emotional manner. These emphasize the idea that the zest for freedom was predominant among all Indians.

A story of one incident during the pre-Independence days in Dhaka brings out effectively the powerful influence of politics on an individual's life. The call for independence was gaining momentum. People of all ages and from all walks of life had plunged into the freedom struggle. In the pursuit of independence people had chosen their own paths. One of the characters, Tha'mma, reacting to a current event, recalls an incident from the freedom struggle. In Bengal those days there were secret societies like Anushilan and Juginter, organisations of militant nationalists with their clandestine networks and homemade bombs with the purpose of liquidating the British officers and policemen who were symbols of oppression and stood in the way of freedom. Hence acts of daring heroism of such secret societies and equally cowardly mercenary acts of betrayal by villagers were well-known in Dhaka, as in the rest of the country. Fascinated and also inspired by stories of heroism, young women like Tha'mma nurtured ambitions of plunging into the struggle through such secret societies. Their desire to participate fully in the freedom struggle was restricted by two factors—their gender and the secrecy with which these societies functioned. Tha'mma had always visualized a militant nationalist as a man with fiery looks, with enormous strength and with a huge moustache. Police raids were frequent in colleges those days. During one such raid, Tha'mma was shocked when one of her frail-looking classmates was arrested. The boy had been a member of a secret society from the time he was fourteen years old. She watched in horrified silence as he was hauled away to prison, a mute spectator of historical circumstances. She idolized him for his tremendous mental strength. The novelist through this incident shows that the struggle had engulfed every one. It focuses on those people who had chosen the militant path in the pursuit of freedom. The boy in *The Shadow Lines* and Joseph D'Costa in *Midnight's Children* significantly have the same ideology. Both of them are fragile looking but possess tremendous mental strength and determination. Both of them are involved in the same kind of militant activities, which is their brand of patriotism.

Amitav Ghosh's *The Circle of Reason* focuses on the imbroglio in the Socialist movement during 1936. Truly committed socialists like Mathur, one of the characters in the novel, were toiling in rural India to create awareness, while pretenders like Mishra, were biding their time to ascend the throne of a new independent India. And when the crunch came in 1947, most of the socialists walked over to the Congress, to lay their hands on the coffers of independent India, destroying the basic fabric of the socialist movement, which ultimately made the Praja Socialist Party extinct. True socialists like Mathur lived and died in obscurity, while theory-speaking pretenders like Mishra were catapulted to the pinnacle of success. The novel is highly critical of such unscrupulous politicians who are the bane of this country.

From a study of the incidents in the novels it is clear that in addition to the burden of history, unethical and unscrupulous politicians by their actions reduce individuals to being mere bearers of history.

The individual as history bearing can be best exemplified through what happens to Dr. Aadam Aziz during the Jallianwallah Bagh carnage. The innocuous Jallianwallah Bagh meeting into which he unwittingly wanders with his attache case turns out into a literal baptism by fire into the freedom movement. A chance sneeze however saves his life. But in the process as he falls on his attache case, the clamp of the bag leaves a permanent bruise on his chest. This wound makes him a literal bearer of history. Dr. Aadam Aziz's wound is symbolic of what happened to millions of Indians during the pre-Independence days.

The Partition: The Individual as History Suffering

As the national movement gained momentum, subversive forces were hacking away at the very ideals on which it had grown. As wiser and saner counsels failed, the spectre of Partition loomed large on the horizon. People of various religions carried away by partisan and misplaced ideologies found it impossible to sink their differences and made the Partition an unavoidable reality. The most traumatic event in the history of modern India was the Partition, unsurpassed in the magnitude of its effect on individuals in the sub-continent. The link between History and the Individual as its sufferer cannot be depicted more vividly than through the tragic drama of the Partition. The Partition was not just a historical event but one which touched the lives of millions of common people throughout the country. The sudden outburst of the simmering animosity between the communities which had co-existed for centuries, tore asunder the basic fabric of the nation, destroying the much-vaunted ideal of religious tolerance. The tragic effect of Partition manifested itself on two fronts—the mindless and bloody violence which set the country ablaze leaving one million people in northern India killed in brutal and primitive manner, and the stupendous mass migration, the largest two-way land migration in history, uprooting hundreds and thousands of long entrenched people and transforming them into refugees overnight. The latter was not merely a geographical dislocation comparable to the migration of the Israelites, it represented a complete disintegration of the lives of millions of people who had to rebuild their lives after a total obliteration of their identities, the helpless sufferers of history. The Partition has had a far-reaching impact on the psyche of the Indian sub-continent, as in the case of the Jews of Nazi Germany; it was a trauma psychologically affecting an entire people. The human dimension has made writers of the sub-continent turn repeatedly to this tragic experience. The theme of Partition dominated the middle phase in the development of the Indian English novel. Even the new generation of writers who have not directly experienced the horrors of Partition found it imperative to touch on such a momentous national catastrophe.

The tremors of Partition are felt even today for the politics of post-Independence India and Pakistan is still enmeshed in the history of Partition. However this distancing has enabled the new writers to project it from a refreshingly new perspective. Although the Partition has found a significant place in the Indian English novels, Rushdie feels that considering the magnitude of the tragedy, the depiction is inadequate both in terms of quality and quantity. He dismisses the books written on it as "anaemic and dull."[17] Given the sincerity and poignancy of many of the fictional depictions of Partition, Rushdie's words may appear an unjustified and harsh indictment. However, it could be taken as a significant indication that different perspectives of this human tragedy are possible.

The earliest novel published on the Partition, Khushwant Singh's *Train to Pakistan* (1965), is located in a village along the newly established Indo-Pakistan border where the violence afoot elsewhere has not yet reached except by report and rumour. The villagers—Muslims and Sikhs—continue to live in harmony, the rhythm of their days set by the arrival and departure of the trains. It is this railway station which is crucially the theatre of all activity in the novel.

> Not many trains stop at Mano Majra. Express trains do not stop at all. Of the many slow passenger trains, only two, one from Delhi to Lahore in the mornings and the other from Lahore to Delhi in the evenings each scheduled to stop for a few minutes. The others stop only when they are held up.[18]

All this has made Mano Majra very conscious of trains. The sound of the arrival and departure of trains regulate the activity of the people of Mano Majra. According to C.N. Srinath, "the train is metaphorically time and consciousness."[19] Then one day a grisly railroad cargo arrives from the west, carrying hundreds of mutilated bodies of Hindus and Sikhs, bound for their new homeland but attacked and murdered enroute by Muslims. The cry for vengeance goes up among a group of young Sikhs who make plans to sabotage the next train to Pakistan, which will carry, in reverse, Muslims to their new homeland. A young Sikh called Jugga, famed in the village as a trouble maker, a thief and a general badmash, gives his life to save the train, for aboard is the Muslim girl he loves. So the train passes into Pakistan and with it the assurance that man possesses an innate nobility even amidst widespread evidence to the contrary.

The next of these historical accounts is Manohar Malgonkar's *A Bend in the Ganges* (1964), a sprawling narrative which depicts not only the aftermath of Independence but the struggle leading to its actuality. The complex plot embraces the lives of a number of characters who represent typical Indians in British India—the wealthy, anglicized Hindus, Muslims, Sikhs, the devout followers of Gandhi, the poor and the downtrodden, oblivious to the imminent disintegration of their lives. When freedom comes they are all caught in the explosion of fury, some beheaded, some castrated, some raped, some rescued, and some unaffected—all by chance it seems. *A Bend in the Ganges* recounts no heroic act to attest to humankind's nobility, for in this fictional world the people—Sikh, Hindus, Muslims, violent or non-violent, rich or poor—are capable of behaviour so selfish, so atrocious, that it renders void all the good they might possess.

Chaman Nahal's *Azadi* appeared in 1975. The narrative traces several Hindu families beset by violence, mishap and misery as they make their way across the Punjab to the comparative safety of Delhi. Of the three novels presenting the Partition tragedy, *Azadi* tries to be most objective. It neither reveals any unexpected nobility among its characters nor shows them as pawns at the mercy of chance in a world ruled by chaos. It is Lala Kanshi Ram who stops amidst the chaos to contemplate the significance of what he and his fellows are suffering, only to conclude that in this most unreal of worlds the true reality exists far beyond the senseless going on of which they are all a part.

Common to all these novels is a sincerity and authenticity of depiction. The tone is uniformly sombre. The writers, having witnessed the carnage of Partition, are more concerned with a realistic presentation of history rather than its imaginative transformation. In contrast, the theme of Partition in the novel of the 1980s moves into a different realm. In an interview, answering a question on contemporary India, Rushdie remarks:

> Yes, it was amazing, It seemed to me what if you had to choose a form as for that part of the world, the form you would choose would be the comic epic. It seemed like the obvious the most natural form and it seemed amazing to me that when you looked at the literature that had been produced about India, it seemed dated and I wondered why these dainty, delicate books were being written about this massive, elephantine place? It was as you'd seen an area of cultivable land and the richest soil in it had never been cultivated. You know that everybody is trying to grow crops in the stony ground around the edges and this wonderful prime soil is just left there.[20]

And from that wonderful prime soil, Rushdie produced *Midnight's Children* (1981) and *Shame* (1983). In these novels Rushdie, born in the year of Partition, moves into a different dimension and in an innovative way represents the Partition. The juxtaposition of the very personal and the historical describing the most tragic events in comic terms gives the event a refreshingly new perspective.

The drama that swept the partitioned land on the evening of 14th August 1947, is reduced to a comic countdown as the hero/narrator's mother's family awaits his birth, praying that it will take place at the moment of Independence. The narrator does mention that outside the Bombay hospital, "the monster in the streets had already begun to celebrate the new myth coursing through its veins." (134) A few minutes later this monster, the narrator reveals, "has begun to roar," while in Delhi a wiry man is saying, "At the stroke of the midnight hour, while the world sleeps, India awakens to life and freedom." (134)

The carnage of the communal war underway a thousand miles to the north, the narrator relegates to the background of the light hearted account of his birth, switching moods, for just a moment to sum up simply—while trains burn in Punjab, with the green flames of blistering paint and the glaring saffron of tired fuel, like the biggest dias in the world. And the city of Lahore too is burning. (134) Then as the monster with its new myth continues to roar and the mythmaker to speak, the sounds of birth join the din and the hero arrives. In fact, he adds to the record of his own birth,

> All over the new India, the dream we all shared, children were being born who were only partially the offspring of their parents—the children of midnight were also the children of the time, fathered, you understand, by history. It can happen especially in a country which is itself a sort of dream. (137)

The reality of the transfer of power is presented in an equally comic and imaginative manner through the game played by Sir Methwold. In a symbolic representation of the Partition, Methwold, a British administrator, is shown to be partitioning his bungalow into five parts. The final discarding of the hairpiece revealing the comic figure of a bald Sir Methwold humorously depicts the hollowness of British pomp and vanity.

The treatment in *Shame* of Partition and its subsequent violence leans even more towards the comic. The religious war set off by Partition, the narrator explains, is the result of a dispute between two groups he calls the "veg and non veg" (61) or the "one godly" and the other "stone godly." Rushdie telescopes all the tumult so carefully reproduced by the earlier novelists into the bombing of a Delhi movie theatre. When some "gardeners of violence" (63) plant a bomb in the theatre belonging to the father of the heroine, she escapes but is left naked and eyebrowless, a condition which Rushdie soon transforms into analogy. "It is the fate of migrants to be stripped of history, to stand naked amidst the scorn of strangers upon whom they see the rich clothing, the brocades of continuity and the eyebrows of belonging." (63) Rushdie continues to derive comedy at the expense of his heroine's nudity, a state disgraceful to Indian women, a condition hardly to be considered comic. How unorthodox is this treatment of feminine modesty becomes more evident when set against one of the scenes in *Azadi*, which depicts a group of Hindu women paraded naked through the streets for the shameful delight of their male communal enemies. No analogies, no comedy here, only the stark record of an ultimate degradation.

Commenting on the refreshingly new technique deployed by Rushdie, Robert L. Ross says, "In both novels Rushdie seizes fragments of the Partition and treats them for the most part as comic, but his intention is always serious."[22] He brings out the Partition carnage with nerve tingling effect through this new technique.

Salman Rushdie's fictional style lends a unique imaginative flavour to the treatment of the theme of Partition. He breaks away from the traditional Indian fictional style of the earlier novels of narrating the events of the Partition in a chronological sequence. He gives a spatial poignance to the estrangement of the communities involved in Partition by his metaphorical style. While the metaphor leads to a land of fantasy and entertainment, the undercurrent which is menacing comes out even more forcefully; the effect is chilling and horrifying. The comic perceptions, the extravagantly metaphorical presentation should not distract us from the undeniable seriousness of Rushdie's analysis of the Partition era. For a brief moment Rushdie seems to be speaking through Joseph D'Costa when he says, "This Independence is for the rich only; the poor are being made to kill each other like flies in Punjab, in Bengal" and continues, "Just now our own people are dying. We got to fight back show the people who to fight instead of each other." (120)

Upamanyu Chatterjee's *English, August*[23] touches but briefly on the saga of Partition. In a couple of pages it catches the essence of the emotional turmoil of a people of a divided nation. It has been one long and lonely trek from Lahore to Madna for Mr. Multani. The dictum that life has to go on finds its best expression in the trials and tribulations of Mr. Multani. The satisfaction of seeing his son through medical college may be a comforting thought but true happiness is elusive as old memories continue to haunt him. The pathetic condition of displaced people, victims of Partition, is conveyed most poignantly when he tells Agastaya Sen the protagonist, "Darshan [his son] is lucky, I would think, he has not been a refugee like me—wanderers clutching only our pasts—we had nothing else." (229) Many years later this emptiness continues to haunt Mr. Multani.

The highly ruthless and frenzied nature of violence between the Hindus and Muslims is conveyed when Mr. Multani contrasts it with the nature of a contemporary riot: "Compared to the Forties, these riots are like fire crackers—hoodlums having their special brand of fun and organizing integration meetings." (229)

It is a sad commentary on those people who now rake up communal passions for their own selfish and vested ends. In spite of having lived during those turbulent times, Mr. Multani considers himself lucky for having experienced the most momentous time in the history of the country. These reminiscences of Mr. Multani are thought-provoking to Agastaya and he is shocked at his own insensitivity: "Multani's father had known the sufferance of colonial rule, but Agastaya and Darshan Multani had not, and unlike John Avery, had not even been particularly inquisitive." (230) It is a sad reflection on the present generation's ineptitude, for whom riots mean a chance of a holiday. Multani's fear that the English "have left behind cultural cripples, incapable of appreciation" (230) may not be far from the truth.

From the foregoing it may be commented that Jugga in *Train to Pakistan*, Debi in *A Bend in the Ganges*, Lala Kanshiram in *Azadi*, Multani in *English, August* and a score of others are all inevitably presented as history suffering.

However the individual as history suffering can be best depicted through Biliquis Hyder in *Shame*. The Partition violence leaves her father dead under bizarre circumstances. Running naked and eyebrowless on the streets, her suffering is beyond description. Her life in Pakistan in spite of all the physical comforts cannot erase the suffering in her mind. Biliquis Hyder's condition is truly symbolic of all those who suffered the inexorable forces of history.

Post-Independence: The Individual as History Creating

In the novel of the Eighties, the post-Independence era is the centre of focus. Being products of this era, the novelists of the Eighties place it under closer scrutiny than the earlier epochs. The protagonists of these novels propel themselves into centre stage, refusing to let their identities be submerged by the forces of history. Stripped of the protective shelter of collective political and social movements, the individual stands alone, attempting to make his mark on the changing face of Indian politics. More often than not, the endeavour ends in disillusionment but the very effort of trying to take charge is a positive step in the right direction.

The long-awaited Independence finally arrived but marred by the horrors of Partition. It left a permanent wound on the psyche of the nation, leading to a significantly different social and political ethos. The freedom struggle had united the politician and the common man. The negative forces which had always been present were submerged in the fervour of nationalism. These negative forces having reared their heads during the Partition now attempted to establish themselves in the ethos of the nation. The post-Independence manipulative, power-hungry politician has changed the very face of politics. The solidarity of the common man and his leader which was such a vital part of the struggle appears distant and in the nature of a myth to the post-Independence generation. Nationalist visions, as a result, now seem no more than a lost ideal, occasionally resuscitated at the convenience of these politicians. Politics is no longer a passionate and selfless commitment but a game of intrigue and underhand surreptitious maneuvrings. In these changed circumstances, the common man perhaps feels it imperative to combat these forces by playing a more dominant role as an individual in an attempt to give history and politics a more humanistic touch. As a result, in the words of Jehanara Wasi, "Rushdie's characters, however bizarre or idiosyncratic, always live in a real world of political pressures. We are able to see in his work, the many complicated ways in which public politics determines private behaviour."[24]

Rushdie's analysis of the different "modes of connection" (285) between history and individual which has been quoted earlier requires to be re-emphasised at this point. He uses the terms "actively-literally, passively-metaphorically, actively-metaphorical and passively-literally." (286) The "passively-metaphorically" and "passively-literal" were the predominant modes in the earlier eras. Although these "modes of connection" are still present in the post-Independence section of the narrative, the "actively-literal" and "actively-metaphorical" now gain preeminence. The multi-faceted dimensions of the connections between history and the individual often operate simultaneously and in conjunction with one another in this phase of the novel. However given the complexity of the post-Independence scenario, it is not easy to specify or categorize the modes as in the earlier sections. The protagonist flits in and out of different modes giving us Rushdie's perception of history as a dynamic and multidimensional force in human life.

Rushdie depicts the individual as occupying a position of

centrality in the scheme of things, both public and personal with his usual flourish. Incident after incident in the narrative reiterates this idea of centrality. No longer is the individual merely connected to history but is shown to attempt an "active-literal" role in the making of history of his times. It is similar to Nietzsche's description about the critical mode of history.

Rushdie's depiction of the major incidents of the post-Independence era has been categorized in this section into two groups—one dealing with incidents confined to the national boundaries, the other with those which go beyond these limits. The modes operating in the first group has been specified by the narrator himself.

In the history of any nation, wars are an important landmark which inevitably touch the lives of the common man to a lesser or greater extent. The complexity of the post-Independence period is further compounded by the three wars in which the country was engaged in quick succession. For the infant nation struggling to find its bearings, the wars proved debilitating both on the economic and psychological arenas. The novel of the Eighties does not merely report the events as detached historical incidents but depicts them through the individual's reaction to these events and their impact on human lives. The idea that, however important historical forces may be, the individual is equally important and can never be relegated to the background is reiterated. The novels seem to be vehemently bent on expounding this perspective.

Rushdie's treatment of the three wars—Indo-China war of 1962, Indo-Pakistan wars of 1965 and 1971—are characteristically innovative. His approach to the depiction of the individual's place in a nation at war throws up an interesting array of possibilities. All the modes of connections established by Rushdie are in operation, at some time or the other. The Indo-China war is presented predominantly in what Rushdie calls the "active-literal" mode. The connection between the nation and the personal events are many and always emphatically made with a flamboyant disregard for realism. It is a technique which Rushdie has mastered brilliantly, leaving on it the stamp of his exuberant imagination.

During the Indo-China war, the Sinai family was in Pakistan then, except for Ahmed Sinai who had refused to move from Bombay. On the afternoon of 9th September, 1962, Amina Sinai was busy trying to cut her verrucas out of her feet with a sharp-ended nail file and elsewhere in New Delhi, Krishna Menon, the then defence minister was reacting equally sharply, threatening to cut off the Chinese in the Himalayan front by the use of force if necessary. A telegram informing her about her husband's heart attack brought the Sinai family back to Bombay on 16th September 1962. Ahmed Sinai in his hour of despair and loneliness was very worried about the Chinese invading India. Back in Bombay, after a gap of four years, Saleem tried to convene the midnight children's conference in a pérsonal attempt to tackle a national emergency. The optimism with which the midnight children assemble mirrors the optimism of the Indian army as it prepared to confront Chinese aggression, both prove equally shortlived and illusory.

Saleem's attempt at convening a conference of the midnight children is prompted by the necessity of bringing together various dissenting forces to tackle a national emergency. And on the personal level, as Neeraja Mattoo remarks, "The emotional integration of the family echoes the fervour of the country's apparent emotional integration in the face of Chinese aggression."[25] The attempt ends disastrously when his compatriots turn against him in a vicious attack: "his mind was no longer a parliament chamber but became a battleground on which the midnight's children tore him apart totally annihilated him on charges of secrecy, prevarication, high handedness and egotism." (357) Simultaneously on October 20th, there was an unprovoked attack by the Chinese army leading to a complete annihilation of the Indian forces at Thag La Bridge. The juxtaposition of the defeat of the Indian army and that of Saleem Sinai is significant. Rushdie seems to suggest that it was not so much the defeat of the Indian army but a weakening of the basic fabric of the nation due to divisive forces.

Undeterred by the crushing attack, Saleem tries to convene another conference between 20th October and 20th November.

But the midnight children started fleeing from him, just when in the high Himalayas, Gurkhas and Rajputs fled in disarray from the Chinese army. The connection between the nation puffing itself, convinced that the defeat of "the little yellow men" (359) was imminent, and the puffing of Saleem's sinus is well made. Thus the most decisive moment of the war is presented in ludicrous juxtaposition with the inflammation of Saleem's sinus. The optimism disease held its sway over Ahmed and Amina. Amina gave away gold bangles and emerald earrings for 'ornaments for armaments' programme, and Ahmed bought war bonds in bushels. In the clutches of the optimism disease, students burnt the effigies of Mao Tse Tung and Chou En Lai. They attacked Chinese shoemakers, curio dealers and restauranteurs. (359) As the Indians headed blindly towards a military debacle, Saleem too was nearing a catastrophe of his own. While his nasal passage was in state of acute crisis, the Indians had attacked under cover of artillery. From 14th November, Nehru's 73rd birthday, the great confrontation with the Chinese forces had begun, but the Indian jawans were routed in Walong. November 20th was a terrible day; just when everyone feared that things would get worse, on 21st November, the Chinese suddenly ceased hostilities and announced cease-fire, bringing much relief in New Delhi. Coincidentally, Saleem's sinus too is cleared on the same day. It takes away from him his prized possession, the power to tune in to the midnight children. However he realizes that the loss has been compensated with the acquisition of an equally powerful sense of smell.

Amitav Ghosh's *The Shadow Lines* deals with the same war in a more realistic manner. The actual incidents of the war are not given as much prominence as in *Midnight's Children*, but the sense of participation of the nation is more predominant. While *Midnight's Children* largely confines itself to the impact of the war on the Sinai family, *The Shadow Lines* presents an entire cross-section of society affected by it. The war is presented in retrospection when sixteen years later, the narrator recalls it in vivid detail. The socio-cultural life of a community was thrown out of gear. The much-awaited ritual visits after Durga Puja were cut short when the narrator's father announced that Nehru had told the army to drive the Chinese back from their border and that war was inevitable. The young narrator at that time little realizing what war meant, was quite excited as he announced the news to his grandmother. An embittered Tha'mma, who had lost her nephew Tridib in the Dhaka riots not very long ago, wanted to teach the Chinese a lesson. The narrator and his friends recalled how as children they had learnt to distinguish between the Indian and Chinese warplanes. Women had donated their bangles and earrings just as Amina and Ahmed Sinai had bought war bonds during the war. Children too had participated and done their mite by standing in street corners taking donation and selling little paper flags. Some kind of euphoria was sweeping over the country, similar to Rushdie's description of the 'optimism disease.' But this soon turned to confusion when the news came that the Chinese had driven the Indian army back. The narrator recalls how as children, they had feared that the Chinese would soon occupy Assam and Calcutta.

Thus the two novels present two different perspectives of the same historical event, emphasizing the connection between history and the individual in their own ways.

The two wars with Pakistan were different in nature from the Indo-China war. They were wars between two communities who had co-existed as one nation before the Partition. The outrage perpetrated by the carnage during Partition left the two communities deeply embittered, so that the slightest provocation could set light to the tinder. The dispute over Kashmir was the spark which resulted in the conflagration of the wars—thus indicating that Indo-Pakistan politics is still embedded in the trauma of Partition. This aspect is most emphatically exemplified in the reactions of Tha'mma in *The Shadow Lines*. She, who had earlier been unable to come to terms with the idea that her native place had now become an alien nation, undergoes a total change of attitude with the gory death of her nephew Tridib at the hands of communal forces. With the outbreak of the war, she donates the chain which she had treasured for thirty-two years. On being questioned about it, she screams: "I gave it to the fund for the war. I had to, don't you see? for your sake, for your freedom, we have to kill them before they kill us, we have to wipe them out . . . this is the only chance, the only one. We're fighting them properly at last with tanks and guns and bombs." (237) In another incident, her intense involvement reaches a frenzy when she shatters the radio with a punch. Her hand had started bleeding, and then very calmly she had announced that she had to get to the hospital because "I mustn't waste all this blood. I can donate it to the war fund." (237)

Through Tha'mma, Amitav Ghosh is able to give a human dimension to the politics of the sub-continent. The Indo-Pakistan war of 1965 is brought into focus by juxtaposing the personal with the historical. Saleem now in Pakistan for some time, hears the news of his grandfather's death and about the arrival of his grandmother in Pakistan. It was then that he started dreaming repeatedly about Kashmir. His dream took him to the Shalimar Bagh, floating in Shikaras, and climbing the hill of Shankara Acharya. Rushdie connects this personal dream of Saleem to what happened when the dream of Kashmir spilled over into the minds of the rest of the population of Pakistan. Saleem found in his private dream of Kashmir in 1965, the common dream of Pakistan. His aunt Alia had infused her old age frustrations into the curricula in her twin institutions, spreading hatred and vengefulness among the young students. The nation's mood of hatred and vengefulness is likewise expressed through a situation brewing within the Sinai family, thus establishing the active-metaphorical mode of connection. This mood of hatred seeped through the windows of the house and took over the hearts and minds of the nation. Confusion thus overwhelmed both the family and the nation. When the war between India and Pakistan finally came, it was wrapped in the same fuddled haze of unreality. Newspapers in Pakistan were reporting about good Indo-Pakistan relations being just around the corner; in reality something else was happening in the disputed territory of Rann of Kutch. On the personal front, the Sinai family thrashed about in the web of their aunt's revenge, while the mill of history continued to grind. It is here that Rushdie lashes out at the distortion of history indulged in by unscrupulous politicians. And as Andrej Gasiorek remarks, "His most pungent satire is directed at the numerous falsification of history in the propaganda enveloping the war between India and Pakistan."[26]

The incidents in the Rann of Kutch thus became the tinder that soon became a raging fire. As in any war, truth first suffered. Both sides started making contradictory statements. Exaggerated accounts of war were given from both sides, one outrageous claim keeping pace with a counter claim. Due to the many untruths reported, the real events of the war were wrapped in a haze. It fed people with all kinds of lies, lulling them into a false sense of security. When reality finally hit them with full force, it dealt a crushing blow both on the body as well as the mind. Saleem now discards the earlier mode of connection and takes on the passive-literal mode. Incidents accumulate to convince him that the pattern of the war was specially designed to annihilate his family. As the narrator points out, "Of the only three bombs to hit Rawalpindi and explode, the first landed on the bungalow in which my grandmother Naseem Aziz and my aunt Pia were hiding under a table; the second tore a wing off the city jail, and spared my cousin Zafar a life of captivity; the third destroyed a large darkling mansion surrounded by a sentried wall" (407); the last was the house in which Saleem and his parents were in residence. Saleem has a providential escape. However in a bizarre accident, the silver spittoon, a family heirloom sent whirling due to the explosion, hits him with full velocity on the back of his head. It obliterates both his consciousness and identity in the same way as the war had inflicted a violent injury on the psyche of the nation.

As in *Midnight's Children*, *Shame* also connects the events of the war with the life of the individuals. It presents the war from the other side of the Indian border. The war is brought into focus through a humorous presentation. Soldiers and all those associated with the war considered themselves lucky to be away from the plains and into the cool of the mountains: "foot soldiers, cooks all rejoiced as they headed for the coolness of the hills. Yara this is luck, na. . . . I won't die in that damn heat."

(77) They went to war not as soldiers but more like holidaymakers. And those who died in the war were promised the perfumed gardens of paradise. The narrative presents contrasting moods. Even as the army morale was high, on the personal front, Rani Humayun was fuming, as she had to postpone her wedding reception. On the other hand Biliquis Hyder and Raza Hyder were extremely happy as hopeful parents. Raza Hyder's victory over a part of the valley of Ansu is attributed to his happiness as an expectant parent. In its own way, this war paradoxically causes a personal rift between the two main characters, Raza Hyder and Isky Harappa, which ultimately ends in disaster for the latter after some time. It also shows that in spite of the war, individuals are preoccupied with their own lives, as can be seen when Biliquis tells Rani. "Never mind this war foolishness, the important news is that I am making a boy to marry your unborn daughter." (78)

The Indo-Pakistan war of 1971 had its origin in the events of the 1970 elections in Pakistan. This election at that time split the country decisively into the East and West wings. The East wings under the leadership of Sheikh Mujabir Rehman started pressurizing for a separate country. As a result the army was pressed into service in order to control insurgency and subversive activity. Commenting on his role in the historical event, Saleem says that "though he had refused to take responsibility, the metaphorical modes of connection refused to abandon him." (420) In the passive-metaphorical mode of connection, Saleem as the Sniffer dog does what he has been ordered to do. As a result he successfully sniffs out Sheikh Mujabir Rehman. The election in Pakistan had led to uneasiness and the deep foundations of this unease lay in the fear of schizophrenia, of splitting, that was embedded in every Pakistani heart. The mass atrocities committed by the Pakistan army resulted in "the biggest migration in the history of the human race" (427) into India. This had forced India into intervening in the war. However the war ended in three weeks, liberating the East wing, thus enabling them to form Bangladesh, paving the way for a re-entry of an old trusted friend Parvati the witch, into his life. Through her, Saleem recollects his name and thus re-discovers his identity after having passed through a long and depressing period of blankness as the Buddha. Through Parvati, Saleem returns to India convinced that "the purpose of that entire war was to reunite him with an old life." (446)

Commenting on Rushdie's presentation of the war David W. Price says, "The Bangladesh war is filtered through the experiences of Ayooba, Shaheed Farooq and Saleem common soldiers . . . their experiences comprise a more accurate history of India. Through this method Rushdie is able to convey the real human tragedy underlying the layers of misrepresentation created by both governments."[27]

What is noteworthy in the depiction of history and the individual in the novel of the Eighties is the unmistakable centrality of the latter. History is never viewed in isolation, but as complementary with the individual's life. As Anita Desai aptly comments, "While an individual's history does not make sense unless seen against its national background, neither does national history make sense unless seen in the form of individual lives and histories."[28]

In the novel *Shame*, Rushdie is highly critical of the people of the East Wing who had forced a split on the nation. Launching a scathing attack on them, the narrator describes them as "savages, breeding endlessly, jungle-bunnies good for nothing but growing jute and rice, knifing each other, cultivating traitors in their paddies." (179) *Shame*, like *Midnight's Children*, recreates the events leading to the civil strife in Pakistan. As in the earlier war, people were fed with all kinds of falsehood and disinformation, and when it was finally announced that the army had surrendered, it stunned the nation into shocked silence. "The traffic stood still in the city streets. The nation's lunch remained uncooked. In the villages, the cattle went unfed and the crops unwatered in spite of the heat." (180) This humiliating defeat seemed to have perpetrated the final shame on the nation. However this division of the nation seemed to have suited the political ambitions of one individual Isky Harappa, as it enabled him to take over the reigns of the partitioned nation.

The manner in which a public event like a war impinges on the life of individuals and, in turn, is affected by these has been explored in the previous section. The complex modes of connection between individuals and events that have shaped the socio-political ethos of the country have been specifically defined by the narrator in the crucial passage enumerating Rushdie's theory of history. The sudden shift into a non-fictional mode in the passage is consciously employed to concretize this theory.

As an exemplification of the passive-metaphorical mode, the narrator selects the episode entitled 'The fisherman's pointing finger.' The fisherman's pointing finger refers to a painting hanging symbolically over the infant Saleem Sinai's crib, showing a fisherman with his finger pointed towards the distant horizon. The narrator interprets it as an indication of the future of both the child and the infant nations. The prodigious appetite of the child resulting in an abnormally quick growth is taken as an indication of the nation's ambitious development programmes. As O.P. Mathur points out, "Saleem's growth mirrors the development of free India. Soon after his birth his huge appetite seemed to be a pointer to India's ambitious five year plans and the large amount of foreign aid, especially American, swallowed by them."[29] The two episodes of the terrifying time of the freeze and the explosion at Walkeswar reservoir establish the passive-literal mode of connection. In a highly imaginative exposition, the personal and the public are brought into focus. Saleem, in the course of the narrative, says that he was responsible for the drastic change in his father's life due to his mere presence. Having lost his place of centrality in the family to baby Saleem, a disillusioned Ahmed Sinai had taken to drink and pursuing an impossible dream of reclaiming land from the sea along with Dr. Narlikar. This project had induced him into spending his money undiscriminatingly. As a result the state had frozen his assets. What happens to Ahmed Sinai is mirrored in a wider sweep, when the country froze the assets of those it presumed were involved in dubious activities. The comment of Dr. Narlikar on this incident touches on rather sensitive issues when he says, "These are bad times Sinai bhai—freeze a Muslim's assets, they say and you make him run to Pakistan, leaving all his wealth behind him, catch the lizard's tail and he'll snap it off! This so-called secular state gets some damn clever ideas." (157)

Characters in *Midnight's Children* are introduced to serve specific purposes. Evie Burns the American girl is introduced into the narrative to suggest the presence of American funds in the country. Her over-bearing and over-confident manner has its obvious associations. The uncertainty over the issue of partitioning of Bombay and widespread drought had brought misery and to add to these woes, the explosions at the Walkeswar reservoir, the main fresh water pipes "which were the city's life lines began to blow fountains into the air like giant steel whales" (268) resulting in an acute water shortage in the city. This breakdown of the water supply system, the narrator says, resulted in the great cat invasion on the Methwold estate, the only place in the city where water was available in plenty. It required the services of Evie Burns with her air gun to be rid of those marauding cats. Saleem's sister, the "brass monkey" who had always resented Evie Burns, makes this an excuse to have a show-down, with her ultimately emerging victorious. With a little stretching of the imagination, the episode can be taken to indicate the country freeing itself from American dominance and interference through their offers of economic aid. This idea is reiterated in Saleem's own words when he says, "I seem to discern the driving force behind their battle to death, a motive far deeper than the mere persecution of cats, they were fighting over me." (270) The connections are obvious again.

The active-metaphorical mode of connection is brought into focus through two incidents that happen to Saleem but exemplifying something deeper in a larger connection. The mutilation of Saleem's middle finger during a fight with his classmates in the course of a school party, which results in a loss of blood, seems to suggest the blood spilled over the issue of Kashmir. In a larger context, it could also suggest the dismemberment of the nations on various other issues. Drawing the connection between the two, the narrator aptly comments, "When I was detached from my finger tip and blood rushed out in fountains, a similar thing happened to history, and all sorts of overwhichthing began pouring all over us, but because history operates on a grander scale than any individual, he took a good deal longer to stitch it back together and mop up the mess." (286) The other incident of mutilation occurs when Mr. Zagallo gives Saleem a monkish tonsure during the course of a human geography class. The demented schoolteacher however draws a brilliant connection between Saleem's face and the map of India, when he explains, "In the face of these ugly ape you don't see the whole map of India? . . . the Deccan Peninsula hanging down." (277) Referring to the stains on Saleem's face, he continues, "These stains are Pakistan! The birthmark on the right ear is the Eastwing, and the horrible stained left cheek, the west." (277) During his virulent attack on the hapless boy, he pulls out a tuft of his hair which resembles a monkish tonsure. This baldness on Saleem's head seems to suggest the problem of Kashmir, an indicator that it may separate from the country through the process of virulent attack both from within and without.

The most important mode, the active-literal, is brought into focus through the incident of the language marchers. The division of Bombay had become a bone of contention between people speaking Marathi and Gujarati. An accident had brought Saleem face to face with one such language march, who demanded to know his loyalties. The terrified Saleem had blurted a few sentences in Gujarati—"Soo che saru che, danda leke maru che." (228) The pro-Marathi language marchers picked up this slogan and in course of time this became a song of war to unleash violence. Thus Saleem says that by giving this slogan, he was directly responsible for the historical partitioning of Bombay. Similarly he holds himself responsible for the war between India and Pakistan, believing that his dream of Kashmir had triggered off a similar dream in the nation's psyche.

As in *Midnight's Children*, so in *Shame*, Rushdie's concern is with contemporary history. As pointed out by Sushila Singh: "*Shame* is a companion piece to *Midnight's Children*. The first was a stupendous evocation of the evolution of India since Independence; *Shame* is about what happened to the other half of the country after 1947. Unfolding the truth about Pakistan, the novel is a queer combination of free flight fairy-tale and a savage political indictment. *Shame* is an expose of the bleak nightmare of Pakistan."[30] Both countries entered the post-Independence era with great hope and aspiration. These expectations were belied in India through manipulative politics, whereas in Pakistan, repressive politics thrust upon the nation resulted in a nightmarish situation. Whatever may have been the shortcomings of a democracy, it does leave open the scope for individual expression and action, as has been seen in Saleem Sinai. An authoritarian political system has place only for the likes of Omar Khayyam Shakil, hovering ineffectually in the background. The repressive forces in Pakistan were not restricted to the political but found expression also through religious fundamentalism and social subjugation of women. These circumstances would make a realistic depiction lacking in force, hence Rushdie's recourse to the powerful fantasy figure of Sufiya Zinobia. Sufiya Zinobia, the 'wrong miracle,' the mentally-retarded daughter of Raza Hyder—the authoritarian leader of a country, again a 'miracle gone wrong,' represents the collective consciousness of a repressed people. Rushdie befittingly chooses a female figure to represent the inter-twined nature of the various forces of repression at work—the political, the religious and the social.

Sufiya Zinobia from her birth is regarded as a misfortune for having shattered the expectation of a male offspring. The burden of shame, laid on Sufiya, increases with the realization of her mental disabilities. The figure of Sufiya gains an increasingly horrifying, almost mythical, stature in the course of the narrative. Her actions exemplify the gathering storm on the political scene. The violence erupts in a small but significant manner when she strangles two hundred and eighteen turkeys belonging to Pinky Aurangezeb. The violence increases when she moves on to strangling human beings and finally reaches its terrible crescendo, when Nishapur, the edifice of shamelessness, is shattered to smithereens.

Many critics have failed to explore the full potential of the symbolic value of the fantasy figure of Sufiya Zinobia. They have under-rated this symbol by making facile connections and restricting her significance to the idea of shame by not viewing the concept of shame in a larger context. The shame of Sufiya is inextricably linked with the shame of the nation, however unacknowledged the latter might be. Like Saleem Sinai, Sufiya too is handcuffed to history. As in *Midnight's Children*, the infant nation and the infant daughter of one of the makers of the nation grow together.

Both nation and Sufiya are victims of an imposed sense of shame, burdened by a shame not of their own actions but forced on them by the larger forces—political, social and religious—which rule their lives. As the narrator comments: "repression is a seamless garment." (173) A nation which represses its women under a patriarchal puritanical code restricting their dress, mobility and sexual freedom, a nation which perpetrates authoritarian rule under the guise of democracy, a nation which imposes inhuman taboos in the name of religion is unabashedly shameless. The shame which should rightfully be felt by the perpetrator is transferred, in a tragic irony, on to its victims. What results is a grotesque and inhuman history and inevitably, the outcome is equally grotesque and inhuman. In such a society, individual action as was attempted in *Midnight's Children* is totally ruled out. It is only a collective will and consciousness which can express the voice of a repressed nation. Sufiya is the grotesque representation of this collective consciousness and dramatically brings out the 'seamless garment of repression' of a nation. Direct social and political criticism is avoided but finds expression in other more subtle ways. The most moving embodiment of Rushdie's power of intense social and political criticism occurs in the passage describing the designs on the eighteen shawls woven by Rani Harappa. Each shawl represents one aspect of repression, thus encapsulating the tragic history of a repressed nation.

> What did the eighteen shawls depict? Locked in their trunk, they said unspeakable things which nobody wanted to hear: the badminton shawl, on which, against a lime-green background and within a delicate border of overlapping racquets

and shuttlecocks and frilly underpants, the great man lay unclothed, while all about him the pink-skinned concubines cavorted . . . the slapping shawl, Islander a thousand times over raising his hand, lifting it against ministers, ambassadors, argumentative holy men, mill owners, servants, friends . . . the hissing shawl, Iskander seated in the office of his glory . . . in silver she revealed the arachnid terrors of the days, when men lied to their sons and angry women had only to murmur to the breeze to bring a fearsome revenge down upon their lovers . . . the torture shawl, she embroidered the foetid violence of his jails . . . the swearing shawl, Iskander's mouth as wide as the abyss, the oaths represented by fowl creatures crawling from his lips . . . the shawls of international shame, Isky grovelling at primrose Chinese feet. . . . Harappa and Shaggy Dog like cruel dogs slitting the throat of an emerald chicken and plucking the feathers from its east wing . . . the election shawls, one for the day of suffrage that began his reign, one for the day that led to his downfall . . . figures breaking seals, stuffing ballot boxes . . . the allegorical shawl, Iskander and the death of Democracy, his hand round her throat, squeezing Democracy's gullet . . . he had taken for her model her memory of an idiot, and consequently innocent, child, Sufiya Zinobia Hyder now Shakil), gasping and empurpled in Iskander's unyielding . . . the autobiographical shawl, the portrait of the artist as an old crone, that self-portrait in which Rani had depicted herself as being composed of the same materials as the house—merging into the fabric of Mohenjo and a fine mist of oblivion clouded the scene; that was the fourteenth shawl . . . the fifteenth—Iskander pointing to the future, only there was nothing on the horizon . . . and the last two were the worst: the shawl of hell . . . her eighteenth shawl and her supreme masterpiece, a panoramic landscape, the hard earth of her exile stretched across the cloth. (191-95)

As M.D. Fletcher sums it up, "direct indictment is levelled at Isky by Rani. Abandoned to the loneliness of the rural Harappa estate, she embroiders a total of eighteen shawls depicting in miraculously fine detail his many crimes."[31]

Sufiya's bouts of increasing violence keep pace with the developments in the nation. The years of shame heaped on the people of the nation are reflected in Sufiya: "Twelve years of unloved humiliation takes its toll." (138) In these twelve years, she had carried the burden of her parents' shame in having borne a female child who is doubly cursed by retarded mental growth after an unfortunate bout of brain fever.

The inaction of her father Raza Hyder over the matter of Pinkie Aurangazeb's turkeys due to an enduring weakness for the glamorous woman leads to Sufiya's first act of violence. In an act of unimaginable violence, she wrenches the heads of two hundred and eighteen turkeys. This incident establishes the link between sharam and violence. The link between the political developments of the nation and its collective consciousness as represented by Sufiya is established more forcefully in subsequent events. As a coup within a military regime establishes a new dictatorship, simultaneously a coup is also staged in Raza Hyder's family. Talvar Ul Haq deposes Haroon Harappa from the affections of his fiance Naveed Hyder and installs himself as the bridegroom. On the day of the wedding there is national as well as family turmoil. The political crisis results in widespread national violence. "Something else was happening that night—under cover of darkness, the people were assembling—that morning the people took to the streets and set fire to motor car, school buses, Army trucks and the libraries of the British Council and the United States Information Service to express their displeasure." (167)

The bizarre marriage which ignores Sufiya's rights as the elder daughter wakes up the somnolent demon in her. This time with increased violence she attacks the bridegroom, almost succeeding in wrenching off his head. Sufiya's outburst is an expression of the rage of a nation taken for granted. It is the year of the general election. Six years of Isky Harappa's tenure has passed and the farcical facade of democracy is maintained by announcing the elections. Once again manipulative and unscrupulous political forces undermine the spirit of democracy, which leaves the people highly agitated. This discontentment of the people is exemplified by the horrendous violence unleashed by Sufiya on the four young men on the streets. Such is the nature of violence unleashed, that it unnerves her father Raza Hyder. As the power-hungry Raza Hyder inflicts on the nation military dictatorship, individual liberty is curtailed when Isky Harappa is imprisoned on concocted charges. Repressive measures are introduced in the name of religion leading to the curtailment of the rights of women; an element of barbarity is introduced citing Islamic laws. Religious extremism has a free reign, forcing God down the throat of an unwilling nation. Raza Hyder, now President, perceives danger from Sufiya to his authority. His design to eliminate her is thwarted by his son-in-law Omar Khayyam Shakil. Sufiya Zinobia, who is now chained and kept drugged in a remote dungeon, symbolizes the chaining and binding of the voice and spirit of the nation. However, on the day Isky Harappa is hanged, Sufiya breaks free and escapes into the countryside, symbolizing the liberation of the people. From now on, Sufiya becomes a frightful and mythical creature. She wanders all over the country, indicating the gathering of the storm in the nation. She moves towards the capital with the single-minded purpose of eliminating the person responsible for perpetrating such shame on the nation. When Raza Hyder flees, the attacks too stop. The story comes a full circle when Sufiya, now the beast, moves towards Nishapur. She is responsible for Raza Hyder's terrible nemesis. The end finally comes when she blows up Nishapur to smithereens, eliminating both shame and shamelessness.

Through his fictional creation of Sufiya, Rushdie portrays a social reality, but at the same time as Joan Rockwell remarks, "also a necessary functional part of social context and paradoxically an important element of social change."[32] Rushdie has effectively used the art of the novel as a weapon to provoke change in a situation which Tariq Ali describes as the "undeniable intellectual, moral and political degeneracy of Pakistan and a dictatorship that can no longer differentiate human beings from animals."[33]

Rushdie's theory of the modes of connection between the individual and history is equally applicable to *Shame*. The modes of connection can be seen to be embodied in the depiction of Sufiya Zinobia. Her role in the novel takes her through the entire gamut—starting as a passive-metaphorical figure, moving on to the active-metaphorical and finally culminating in an active-literal role. Representing the collective consciousness of the people, she exemplifies the effects of a repressive socio-political environment, and as such symbolizes the passive-metaphorical mode. Her mental retardation, the stunting of her as an individual is a symbolic manifestation of the malady afflicting the nation. The active-metaphorical mode of connection which finds a reflection of things done to or by her comes into focus in one striking incident. The violence that she unleashes on Talvar Ul Haq during the wedding reflects the violence unleashed on the streets of the nation by a people frustrated at the never-ending political turmoil. Her potential to play the active-literal role reaches a crescendo in the later part of the novel. The terrible violence perpetrated by her results in Raza Hyder's flight from the capital, thus marking a decisive turn in the history of the nation. In a larger context the narrative emphasizes that this violence is not limited to the family but deliberately creates a vision of a country in flames. It is through violence that the oppressed nation attempts to take charge of its own destiny, creating history through a process of destruction. In other words, as Timothy Brennan says, Rushdie's writing is "dedicated to recovering individual expression and to weakening the power that various governments as 'sales persons' hold over US."[34]

The active-literal mode of connection finds its most powerful expression in the formation of the midnight children's conference. As Sufiya in *Shame* represents a collective consciousness although a violent one, so also the midnight children's conference exemplifies a national consciousness attempting to function on more democratic lines to create history. Saleem Sinai uses his supra powers to convene the midnight children's conference with the belief that the congregation of responsible and enlightened citizens could play a decisive role to create a more positive history for the newly independent nation.

The depiction of the historical Hazaratbal incident can be taken as a clear instance of the pre-occupation of the novel of the Eighties with the interconnection of history, politics and the individual. The episode gains more significance because it occurs in both *Midnight's Children* and Amitav Ghosh's *The Shadow Lines*. Rushdie's treatment of the episode is rather cursory; his interest seems rather to re-emphasise the connection between the nation's history and that of his family, than to explore the significance of the situation. He implies that his grandfather Aadam Aziz could be responsible for the disappearance of the holy Relic, "as a revenge upon God by a father who had lost his son," (333) Aadam Aziz dies in Kashmir five days before the relic is recovered. Soon after, the head of the nation Nehru too passes away.

Amitav Ghosh's treatment is not only more detailed and imaginative but also more significant in its understanding of the role of politics in the sub-continent, and its effect on history and the individual. He suggests that the politics of the nations of the sub-continent are inseparable, that incidents in one reverberate in other parts of the sub-continent. And as Sushila Singh says, "Drawing heavily from his personal experiences, he brings in collision personal and public happenings with locales shifting and merging between Calcutta, London and Dhaka."[35] The volatile nature of political forces has turned the sub-continent into a tinderbox ready to ignite at the slightest provocation. The Hazaratbal episode is used by Amitav Ghosh to expose the fragile nature of communal harmony, its vulnerability to manipulative politics. Tracing the history of the Mu-i-Mubarak, Amitav Ghosh shows that it had grown into a symbol of unity among the various communities of Kashmir. The shrine sheltering the holy relic had become a great centre of pilgrimage; multitudes of people, Kashmiris of every religious faith, would throng to the shrine on occasions when the relic was displayed. Over the centuries, the shrine became a symbol of the unique and distinctive culture of

Kashmir. The disappearance of the sacred relic had spontaneously brought the people of Kashmir together in a feeling of shared loss. As Amitav Ghosh comments, "There is a note of surprise, so thin is our belief in the power of syncretic civilizations—in the newspaper reports that tell us that the theft of the relic had brought together the people of Kashmir as never before." (225) This was possible through the efforts of people like Maulana Masoodi, an authentic but unsung hero. In a small but significant gesture, the Maulana persuaded the demonstrators to march with black flags instead of green. Rumours and mischievous political and religious forces however soon disrupted this collective display of mourning. There were demonstrations and meetings in both East and West Pakistan and it was declared that the theft of the relic was an attack upon the identity of the Muslims. Local disgruntled communal forces were quick to capitalize on these insidious pronouncements. The edifice of unity was shattered, resulting in large scale rioting not only in the country but also in the other parts of the sub-continent.

The tangled web of communal politics in the sub-continent entraps Tridib, an important character in *The Shadow Lines*. Significantly he is gruesomely butchered to death, not in his own country but on the streets of Dhaka, aflame with the repercussions of the Hazratbal incident in distant Kashmir. Surrounded by a rioting mob, Tridib yet attempts to rescue his elderly uncle and faces the consequence.

Tridib's heroic attempt, and its tragic failure, symbolizes the positive potential of the active-literal mode, as does Saleem Sinai's aborted endeavour to unite the midnight's children similarly. Alu in Amitav Ghosh's *The Circle of Reason*, a victim of political forces that have hounded him out of his country, fails in his brave attempt to create history in far away al-Ghazira. However, Agastaya in Upamanyu Chatterjee's *English, August* emerges victorious in his attempt to leave a mark on the wretched conditions of an obscure and oppressed tribal village.

The narrator of *Midnight's Children* mourns the failure of the active-literal mode. "The active-literal passed us by," he says. (286) However, to dismiss the attempts of Saleem or Sufiya or Tridib or Agastaya as failures does not do justice to the courage and potentiality for positive action that they exemplify. The new novel of the Eighties ultimately holds out a ray of hope in its depiction of the multifarious connections between history, politics and individual. The individual has the determination and will to rise above all disruptive political and communal forces to forge a new and more positive history. And as Aruna Srivastava aptly comments, "such a view of history does not allow humans to hide behind ideas of destiny or fate."[36]

Saleem Sinai is the embodiment of the new individual. In spite of the many physical mutilations he suffers he is still determined to combat the forces of history. History's oppression does act as a deterrent in his attempt to create history. And in the process enables him to find a new identity for himself and his nation.

NOTES

1. Salman Rushdie, *Midnight's Children* (1980; New York: Avon Books, 1982).
2. K. Raghavendra Rao, "The Novel as 'Chutney': Unriddling Salman Rushdie's *Midnight's Children*," *Perspectives on Indian Fiction in English*, ed. M.K. Naik (New Delhi: Abhinav, 1985), p. 159.
3. Friedrich Nietzsche, "On the Uses and Disadvantages of History for Life," *Untimely Meditations*, trans. R.J. Hollingdale (Cambridge: Cambridge Univ. Press, 1983), p. 72.
4. David W. Price, "Salman Rushdie's 'Use and Abuse of History' in *Midnight's Children*," *ARIEL: A Review of International English Literature*, 25:2 (1994), p. 93.
5. Walter Allen, *Reading a Novel* (London: Phoenix House, 1940), pp. 18-19.
6. Ralph J. Crane, "The Chutnification of History," *Inventing India: A History of India in English Language Fiction* (London: Macmillan, 1992), p. 171.
7. Salman Rushdie, interview by Gordon Wise, *Gentleman*, Feb. 1984, p. 59.

8. B.K. Joshi, "It may be long, but it is not overwritten," *The Times of India*, 1 Nov. 1981, p. 8.
9. Wise, p. 57.
10. Wise, p. 57.
11. Niel Ten Kortenaar, "*Midnight's Children* and the Allegory of History," *ARIEL*, 26:2, 1995, p. 41.
12. Neeraja Mattoo, "Indianness in *Midnight's Children*: Rushdie's View of an 'Amnesiac Nation,'" *The Indian Novel in English: Essays in Criticism*, ed. Ravi Nandan Sinha and R.K. Sinha (Ranchi: Ankit, 1987), p. 67.
13. Tariq Rehman, "Politics in the Novels of Salman Rushdie," *The Novels of Salman Rushdie*, ed. G.R. Taneja and R.K. Dhawan (New Delhi: Prestige, 1992), p. 102.
14. Amitav Ghosh, *The Shadow Lines* (1988; New Delhi: Ravi Dayal Publisher, 1992).
15. Amitav Ghosh, *The Circle of Reason* (New Delhi: Roli Books International, 1986).
16. Novy Kapadia, "Imagination and Politics in Amitav Ghosh's *The Shadow Lines*," *The New Indian Novel in English: A Study of the 1980s*, ed. Viney Kirpal (New Delhi: Allied, 1990), p. 201.
17. Salman Rushdie, *The Times of India*, 1 Nov. 1981, p. 8.
18. Khushwant Singh, *Train to Pakistan* (New Delhi: Ravi Dayal Pub, 1988), p. 18.
19. C.N. Srinath, "'The Writer as Historical Witness: Khushwant Singh's *Train to Pakistan* and Chaman Nahal's *Azadi*," *The Literary Criterion*, 25.2 (1990), p. 60.
20. Salman Rushdie, interview, "Author from Three Countries," by Michael J. Kaufman, *New York Book Review*, 13 Nov. 1983, p. 3.
21. Salman Rushdie, *Shame* (1983; Calcutta: Rupa, 1983).
22. Robert L. Ross, "The Emerging Myth: Partition in the Indian and Pakistani Novel," *ACLALS Bulletin*, 7.4: 1986, p. 3.
23. Upamanyu Chatterjee, *English, August: An Indian Story* (1988; New Delhi: Rupa, 1994).
24. Jehanara Wasi, Review of *The Circle of Reason*, *Indian Horizons*, Vol. 36, No. 1-2, 1987, p. 53.
25. Mattoo, p. 66.
26. Andrzej Gasiorek, *Post War British Fiction: Realism and After* (London: Edward Arnold, 1995), p. 168.
27. Price, p. 104.

28. Anita Desai, "Where Cultures Clash by Night," *Book World: Contemporary Literary Criticism*, Vol. 23 (Detroit: Gale Research Co., 1983), p. 365.
29. O.P. Mathur, "A Metaphor of Reality: A Study of the Protagonist of *Midnight's Children*," *Indian English Literature since Independence*, ed. K. Ayyappa Paniker (New Delhi: The Indian Association for English Studies, 1991), p. 73.
30. Sushila Singh, "*Shame*: Salman Rushdie's Judgement on Pakistan," *Studies in Indian Fiction in English*, ed. G.S. Balaram Gupta (Gulburga: JIWE, 1989), p. 14.
31. M.D. Fletcher, "Rushdie's *Shame* as Apologue," *The Journal of Commonwealth Literature*, 21.1 (1986), p. 123.
32. Joan Rockwell, "Fact in Fiction," *The Use of Literature in the Systematic Study of Society* (London: Routledge and Kegan, 1974), p. 4.
33. Tariq Ali, "Where is Pakistan Going?" *The Illustrated Weekly of India*, 16 Oct. 1983, p. 17.
34. Timothy Brennan, "*Shame*'s Holy Book," *The Journal of Indian Writing in English*, 16.2 (July 1988), p. 222.
35. Sushila Singh, "Double Self in Amitav Ghosh's *The Shadow Lines*," *Quest for Identity in Indian Writing*, Part 1, Fiction, ed. R.S. Pathak (New Delhi: Bahri, 1992), p. 135.
36. Aruna Srivastava, "The Empire Strikes Back: Language and History in *Shame* and *Midnight's Children*," *ARIEL*, 20.4 (1989), p. 70.

Search for Identity

Since times immemorial the search for identity has been an integral part of the Indian consciousness. Under the impact of the inherent spiritual leanings of Indian culture, this search has traditionally taken the shape of a spiritual quest. Innumerable stories in the oral narrative tradition survive to substantiate this claim.

In the first phase of its development, the Indian English novel was closely associated with the national movement. Consequently the concern with an individual search for identity was submerged under a broader concern with the national identity. The national identity having been established through independence, there was now scope for foregrounding the search for identity at the individual level. The post-independence decades thus see the increasing prominence of this theme. The search for identity is regarded widely as being the major concern of the twentieth century European novel. It is an outgrowth of the existential philosophy which preoccupied the European intellectuals of the age. Existential philosophy is obsessed with the malaise of life, a sense of spiritual vacancy, and attempts to fathom some meaning from the barrenness. Such concerns do not appear to be of great significance given the Indian socio-economic contexts where survival itself is problematic. Consequently, the search for identity in the Indian English novel, although sharing its nomenclature with the European novel, takes on a different form.

The first clear treatment of this theme is found in Raja Rao's *The Serpent and the Rope*. The search for identity in this novel takes on the age-old form of a spiritual quest which takes the protagonist to the ultimate step of merging his self into an omni divine consciousness. The treatment retains the popular trappings of this ancient theme—the river symbolising the flow of life, the inevitable journey of the grihastha, and ultimately enlightenment through the guru. Although R.K. Narayan's *The Guide* differs significantly from Raja Rao's metaphysical treatment, it too takes recourse to a spiritual solution. After these initial explorations, the search for identity takes on a different shape in a group of novels dealing with the problem of cultural alienation. The focus moves from the spiritual and metaphysical to more contemporary reality. Even after independence, the legacy of the colonial past continued to impinge on the Indian consciousness, giving rise to an inevitable clash of cultures. The search for identity thus takes on the particular form of an East-West encounter, leading to a range of solutions, which includes marriage and renunciation as discussed in Chapter 1. Arun Joshi's novels continue the idea of a spiritual quest under a different guise. Disgust with the superficialities of upper-class urban existence propels the protagonist into a search for roots.

The change of consciousness and perceptions which gave the novel of the Eighties a significantly different form than its predecessors has been discussed in Chapter 1. These changes have played a decisive role in shaping the thematic concern of the novel of the Eighties as shown in the Chapter, "History, Politics and the Individual." The search for identity mirrors the compelling realities of a cosmopolitan consciousness.

This chapter attempts to explore the significantly new form in which this theme is presented in the novels studied.

I

The search for identity in the novel of the Eighties finds its most complex expression in *Midnight's Children*. The complexity is an inevitable outcome of the sheer expanse of the novel with its multitudinous experiences. The protagonist's search for identity moves parallel to a similar effort of the newly born nation. As has been pointed out in chapter 1, the protagonist is consciously presented as being "Handcuffed to history, my [his] destinies indissolubly chained to those of my [his] country." (3)

The search for identity on the part of the protagonist is marked into three distinct phases. The first phase is one in which the protagonist undergoes a crisis of identity due to several factors. This leads to the second phase of negation and total loss of identity. The final phase is one of reconstruction as the protagonist attempts to establish an identity on his own terms.

Much has been made of the connection between Rushdie's expatriate status and his interest in the quest for an integrated identity. According to R.S. Pathak "The treatment of dispossessed character's plight is born to a great extent, of Rushdie's personal experiences. . . . Rushdie's novels faithfully delineate the predicament of the people with a partial identity."[1] But Saleem Sinai is no dislocated Expatriate. His predicament grows out of the realities of contemporary Indian existence. This fact is established through the manner in which Rushdie himself emphasises the connection between his protagonist and the nation. The expatriate's crisis is primarily due to a cultural and geographical dislocation. On the other hand, Saleem's sense of disorientation is due to the compelling realities of contemporary life. Critics have noticed a certain kinship between *Midnight's Children* and Gunter Grass's *The Tin Drum*. Deval Dharkar comments: "Both books present an omniscient adult consciousness trying to come to terms with the collapse of history."[2]

The moment of his birth itself is the first significant indication of the crisis of identity which will plague him through much of his life. The choice of that moment to co-incide with the birth of an independent India is a deliberate narrative device, blatant in its artifice. As M.K. Naik aptly comments: "His birth on the stroke of midnight on the day which marks the great divide between colonial and independent India is itself symptomatic of his identity crisis . . . being a midnight's child he is born with a basically divided character."[3] Other factors, too, have contributed to the protagonist's sense of fractured identity. At birth in Dr. Narlikar's nursing home, Mary Pereria, who identifying with her boyfriend Joseph's D'Costa's socialist ideals exchanges babies born into two homes belonging to the opposite ends of the social and economic spectrum. Thus Saleem Sinai the son of poor parents finds a home in the affluent Sinai family. This switching of babies, a device obviously borrowed from popular Hindi movies is a blatant device to reiterate the protagonist's confusion of identity: equally blatant is the saddling of the child with a multiplicity of parent figures. As Saleem Sinai wryly comments, "Giving birth to parents has been one of my stranger talents." (243) Mother figures abound—his real mother Vanitha, his putative mother Amina, the nurse Mary Pereria, his aunt Pia; even more plentiful are the father figures, the English man William Methwold, Wee-Willie-Winke, the street singer, Dr. Schaapstaker, the German snake doctor who saves his life when still a child, his uncle Zulfikar, Hanif Aziz, his maternal uncle, the snake charmer, Picture Singh and of course Ahmed Sinai. Such a nebulous inheritance will inevitably cause a confused and fragmentary identity.

From birth Saleem Sinai is caught between dual expectations. Ahmed Sinai's unborn child brings with him the burden of a prophecy. Since this child is switched at birth, the protagonist enters the scene as Ahmed Sinai's son and carries the weight of this prophecy. Hailed as the Mubarak, the child grows up with illusions of his own divinity, which is not shared by his family members. He alone takes the predictions seriously and believes that "voices will guide him." (195) The hyper-imaginative boy fantasises that voices are calling out to him, and immediately identifies himself grandiosely with the Prophets Moses and Mohammed. Knowing that the voices had urged Prophet Mohammed to write the Quran, Saleem envisages an equally impressive future for himself. He saw "The shawl of genius fluttering down like an embroidered butterfly, the mantle of greatness settling upon my shoulders." (192) Saleem's pompous illusions are shattered, when he is charged with blasphemy by his family and even soundly beaten by his father resulting in permanent deafness in the left ear. Saleem moans the passing away of "being certain of myself for the first time in my life" and plunging into "constant doubts about what I was for." (195) The crisis of identity has truly begun.

Even as Salem Sinai is attempting to grapple with the role of

Messiah thrust on him by a prenatal prediction, he is simultaneously burdened with a second expectation very different in nature. Nehru's words

> You are the newest bearer of that ancient face of India which is eternally young. We shall be watching over your life with the closest attention; it will be, in a sense, the mirror of our own. (143)

inspire him. Saleem's attempts to reconcile the dual expectations mirror the crisis of identity of a nation, striving to balance traditional religious attitude with the new secular ideals. Being rejected in his attempt to project himself in the traditional Messiah role, Saleem modifies it in keeping with the secular ethos, that the new nation is trying to establish. The voices heard in the washing chest which had inspired him, and in his unsuccessful attempts to project himself as a Messiah are now transformed onto the clamouring voices of a secular independent India. The accident in the washing chest that had nudged his mind's door open to certain disembodied sensations is transformed into distinct voices after another bicycle accident. Having thus made the abandoned clock tower his headquarters for his daily inter action with the midnight children, he becomes a radio transmitter into which the children of midnight start tuning in.

The precocious nine-year-old Saleem Sinai begins his attempt to form a midnight children's conference with a considerable hope. Fired with a sense of purpose, Saleem wishes to use the supra powers of the midnight children in the service of this impoverished nation. He wants it to be "a loose federation of equals with all the points of view given full expression." (263) As in the earlier instance, his hopes are shattered. Discord soon sets into the midnight children's conference with the entry of Shiva, the real Saleem Sinai and now the leader of a gang of street urchins. Shiva makes his intentions clear when he says, "gangs ought to have gang bosses" (263); his immediate desire is to take charge of the midnight children's conference and to be its leader. Shiva with his unashamed philosophy, "You got to get what you can" (264) is the symbol of the cynical and materialistic approach to life which can undo the vision of a secular India. Dieter Riemenschneider observes "Shiva is condemned to a life of poverty and crime; he rejects Saleem's search for the purpose and meaning of their lives because poverty leaves no room for idealistic philosophising."[4] Thus looking at Shiva's aggressive stance and predicament, his pronouncements may not be too shocking. But disturbed by Shiva's dismissal of purposefulness as the privilege of the rich, Saleem begins to doubt his own role in the conference. Deprived of support from either his parents or the midnight children pre-occupied with worldly and selfish interests, Saleem's faith in his own convictions begin to waver. He is caught in a flurry of conflicting emotions; the Prime Minister's words which he had treasured so far, now appear tinged with a different and more cynical significance. The attitude of the midnight children had a frustrating effect on Saleem. They in fact reflected the national prejudices and differences. In other words, they revealed in miniature the dissensions prevalent in this country and so in a tragic paradox, they are like the mirror that the Prime Minister had so hopefully referred to. Though nine-year-olds were talking of identity, purpose and the role of the individual, none of the deliberations bore fruit as the midnight children were too preoccupied with selfish and worldly desires. Thus Saleem Sinai feels increasingly frustrated and alienated, a prey to uncertainty regarding his identity.

The protagonist's appearance is presented with a sardonic, almost metaphysical wit, characteristic of Rushdie. In an apparently violent yoking together of heterogeneous elements Saleem Sinai's face is represented as bearing a remarkable resemblance to the map of India. When asked in an interview how the idea had struck him, Rushdie's reply was:

> It was a comic notion which struck when I was looking at the map. I saw it as a nose hanging into the sea with a drip off the end of it, which is Ceylon. It was another way of making flesh the idea of Saleem's link with the country.[5]

This aspect is illustrated graphically by a cynical school teacher's ridicule of Saleem Sinai's appearance; "In the face of these ugly ape you don't see the whole map of India? . . . the Deccan peninsula hanging down." (277) Referring to the stains on Saleem's face he continues: "These stains are Pakistan! These birthmarks on the right ear is the East wing; and these horrible stained left cheek, the west." (277) His fragmented personality is manifest in his grotesque physical appearance, "the unseemly birth marks spreading to his western hairline, his rampant cucumber of a nose" (124) "temples like stunted horns, his unblinking eyes and irretrievably bowed legs." (149) In the process of growth, his appearance becomes increasingly even more grotesque, as he is subjected to a series of personal mutilations. The first mutilation he is when his father's angry blow leaves him permanently deaf in his left ear. And a more painful blow occurs when his school teacher Mr. Zagallo creates a monkish tonsure during a virulent attack on the hapless young school boy's appearance. At his school socials, in the course of an altercation with his envious schoolmates, he loses the top third of his middle finger. The most significant of these mutilations in this stage of his search for identity occurs much later, when he is brained by the silver spittoon, during the 1965 Indo-Pakistan war:

> Something twisting turning somersaulting down, silver as the moonlight, a wondrously worked silver spittoon inlaid with lapis lazuli . . . plummeting towards me . . . a feeling at the back of my head . . . all Saleems go pouring out of me . . . wiped clean as a wooden writing chest, brained by my mother's silver spittoon. (409-10)

This results in a debilitating loss of memory even to the extent of forgetting his own name. As R.S. Pathak points out that the loss of name is "an analogue suggesting Saleem's identity crisis."[6] With this loss of memory and name, Saleem's identity crisis moves on to the next phase of total negation.

Since the novelist has been at obvious pains to link his protagonist with the nation, it is logical to conjecture that the physical mutilations have a larger significance. They suggest the dismemberment of the nation. The partition with its tragic hacking of the nation, the increasing fragile and tenuous hold on Kashmir with the constant threat of a complete break away, the conflict with Bangladesh all are indicators of a nation disintegrating. Mutilations need not be confined to merely the geographical; it can be extended to include a collapse of cordial international relations. Thus Saleem's personal crisis runs parallel to the crisis of the nation, as it attempts to find a stable footing.

The sense of dislocation which haunts Saleem throughout his life finds another externalisation in his narrative. His constant and disjointed physical movements from one location to the other emphasise his fragmentary identity. As he grows into adulthood, the increasing pressure on his integrated identity, is reflected in the constant to and fro movements. Beginning with a sudden shift to his Uncle Mustafa Aziz's house in childhood, the movement gains momentum when Saleem is constantly shuffled between India and Pakistan. This frenetic shift of location is a predominant feature of the novel of the Eighties, and is in striking contrast to the static nature of the earlier Indian-English novels. While the narratives of R.K. Narayan's novels rarely ever stretch beyond the confined limits of Malgudi, the novel of the Eighties is marked by trans-national and even trans-continental movements. The search for identity in an increasingly complex contemporary world demands an unshackling of the narrative from a single geographical location.

At the age of ten, Saleem's family is split as his mother shifts with her two children to Pakistan, leaving behind her husband who stubbornly refuses to try a new life away from India. This division in the family, the divided loyalties which split them, encapsulates the predicament of many Indian Muslims. Any narrative purporting to deal with the historical and social realities of life on the sub-continent cannot fail to focus on this compelling aspect of this reality. For four years, Saleem is a reluctant resident of Pakistan, unable to identify with the socio-politico ethos of the newly emerged nation. The whimsicalities of a military dictatorship, the flimsy and fragile nature of the entire political system are graphically communicated in the episode of the "Pepperpots":

> General Zulfikar described troop movements; I moved pepperpots symbolically while he spoke. . . . I shifted salt-cellars and bowls of chutney; This mustard jar is company A occupying head post office, There are two pepperpots surrounding a serving spoon, which means company B had seized the airport. With the fate of the nation in my hands, I shifted condiments and cutlery, capturing empty biriani-dishes with water glass, stationing salt-cellars . . . in the movements performed by pepper pots etcetera, one table-ornament remained uncaptured: a cream-jug in solid silver, which, in our table-top coup, represented the Head of State, President Iskander Mirza; for three weeks, Mirza remained President. (348-49)

A state of uncertainty pervades these four years of Saleem's life, consequently leaving him unsure of his moorings. Throughout his childhood, he had been sustained by his self-created identity as a member of the midnight children's conference. This identity had been snatched away, when on entering Pakistan, the transmitter linking him to his fellow midnight children had been significantly jammed. Saleem's relief at returning to India proves short-lived, as he soon realises much to his consternation that the snapped ties with the midnight children cannot be reinstated. The loss of this particular identity forged by Saleem turns out to be permanent, when he undergoes a sinus operation; which leaves the transmitter permanently disabled. This loss is, however, compensated by a sudden and equally miraculous gift—a sense of smell:

> I had been drained—although no voices spoke in my head, and never would again—there was one compensation; namely that, for the first time in my life I was discovering the astonishing delights of possessing a sense of smell. (366)

a power with which he was "capable of smelling sadness and joy, of sniffing out intelligence and stupidity with my [his] eyes closed." (370) Although apparently miraculous this new gift is a precursor to a later stage of degrading dehumanisation, when Saleem is reduced to the status of a sniffer dog.

The second stage of Saleem's search for identity unfolds when the family seems to have resolved its problem of divided loyalties, when it decides to shift fully to Pakistan, with an enticing vision of a new life in the "Land of the Pure." However, the sense of dislocation continues to haunt the protagonist as the crisis of identity moves inexorably to a state of total negation. The crisis takes place on two fronts—the personal in his suddenly changed relation to his sister, and the social in his failure to reconcile the ideal vision of Pakistan with its murky reality. The relationship with Jamila, his sister, creates in him a dual sense of confusion. Jamila, who is now Jamila Singer, the darling of the masses, dislodges him from centre stage, a position which he thought was his birthright. The unexpected rapid decline in his fortunes leaves him even more confounded. Saleem's predicament is worsened with the horrible realisation that he is in love with his own sister. Taibibi,. a five hundred and twelve year old prostitute, an expert at imitating smells brings to the fore the horrifying truth of Saleem's incestuous love for his sister: "I learned the unspeakable secret of my love for Jamila Singer from the mouth and scent glands of that most exceptional of whores." (382) His fatal attraction for Jamila Singer, perhaps, was due to what he saw in her: the hopes of his own life, the fulfilment of his most private dreams. On the socio-political front, the confusion further aggravates when Saleem feels that he was adrift, disoriented amidst an infinite number of falseness, unrealities and lies, in a land "Where truth is what it is instructed to be." (389)

The sense of purposelessness is conveyed when Saleem wanders aimlessly on the streets of Karachi picking up women of the streets. While Jamila sang of holiness and love-of-country, "I picked up the women of the street. . . . And eventually I nosed out the whore of whores whose gifts were a mirror of my own." (381)

Corrupt politicians and the antics of their unscrupulous sons, discord within the family, his incestuous longing for Jamila Singer, and deterioration in his own behaviour are part of his troubled experience during his stay in Pakistan. One horror followed another, leaving him with the feeling that "the years were of diseased reality." (403)

To reiterate his point of being inextricably handcuffed to history, he sees in the Pakistani aggression on Kashmir an expression of his own unfulfilled longings of the beautiful state. The callousness of both governments towards human life, the deliberate disinformation practised by both nations as well as his disturbing love for his sister leave him in a state of acute depression culminating in a death wish. "I went in search of friendly, obliterating, sleep-giving, paradise-bringing bombs. . . . I rode the night-streets of the city, looking for death." (407) While death is elusive to him, the war paradoxically claims the other members of the family. He watches with horror his family home with all the members in it explode in a bomb attack. This explosion releases a "family heirloom inlaid with lapis lazuli" (409) which had lain hidden in a green tin trunk. The flying spittoon hits Saleem with such velocity that it obliterates his memory and along with it, all the identities he had acquired in the eighteen years of his life:

> Saleems go pouring out of me, from the baby who appeared in Jumbo-sized front-page baby snaps to the eighteen-year-old with his filthy dirty love pouring out goes shame and guilt and wanting to please and needing to-be-loved and determined to find-a-historical-role and growing-too-fast, I am free of Snotnose and Stainface and Baldy and Sniffer and Mapface and washing-chests and Evie Burns and language marchers, liberated from Kolynos kid and the breasts of Pia mumani and Alpha-and-Omega, absolved from the multiple murders of Homi Catrack and Hanif and Aadam Aziz and Prime Minister Jawaharlal Nehru, I have shaken of five-hundred-year old whores and confessions of love at dead of night, free now, beyond caring, . . . brained by my

> mother's silver spittoon. (409-10)

Totally devoid of memory, Saleem leads a virtual vegetable existence for six long years in a hospital. Michael Murphy's comment on the importance of a name, "The name surrounds us like a cloak. . . . A name can shape a life"[7] is a reflection of Saleem's helplessness. The crisis of identity has reached a state of total negation. A tragic transformation takes place in a person who had pretensions of being a hero. A recognition of Saleem's miraculous sense of smell brings him yet another identity—the inhuman degrading one of a sniffer dog. The internal dissensions between the two wings of Pakistan flare up into a full-fledged war in the sub-continent over the creation of Bangladesh. Saleem is now drafted into the CUTIA unit of the army to sniff out insurgents in East Pakistan. The fact that he merges himself into this identity without a protest is a clear indication of the depth of Saleem's degradation in the course of his quest for identity. The three young soldiers drafted along with him give him one more identity, that of "buddha," which means old man, "because there hung around him an air of great antiquity. The buddha was old before his time." (418) The narrator, also commenting on it, says:

> The identity of the buddha carries with it a certain ambivalence. The Urdu word "buddha," meaning old man, is pronounced with the D's hard and plosive. But there is also Buddha, with soft tongued D's, meaning he-who-achieved-enlightenment-under-the-bodhi tree. (418)

While in his physical appearance he is buddha, an old man, in his attitude too he seems to have all the trappings of the Buddha, the enlightened one. The Buddha like detachment is merely an illusion. While the Buddha's detachment was the by-product of an elevated consciousness, Saleem's was due to a more resigned submission. "Emptied of history, the buddha learned the arts of submission, and did only what was required of him." (419) The narrative mode suddenly shifts to the third person as if to underscore the idea of the total negation of Saleem's identity. Thus during the Bangladesh war serving as an agent of the Pakistani government in his role of the sniffer dog, Saleem becomes an unconscious collaborator of the atrocities on human life and dignity perpetrated by the army. Saleem, who had always hungered for centrality, resigns to living in a vacuum, unquestioningly pursuing his duties as a sniffer dog. However the narrator protagonist is almost gloating to Padma: "Yes Padma, when Mujib was arrested, it was I who sniffed him out, it's easy when you've got the smell." (425)

In a passage reminiscent of the encapsulated history of Pakistan presented through Rani Harappa's shawl knitting in *Shame*, the gruesome reality of civil war is expressed through the horrified eyes of the three young soldiers:

> Soldiers entering women's hostels without knocking; women, dragged into the streets, were also entered, and again nobody troubled to knock . . . roadside ditches filling up with people who were not merely asleep—bare chests were seen, and hollow pimples of bullet holes. Ayooba Shaheed Farooq watched in silence . . . our soldiers-for-Allah, our worth-ten-babus jawans held Pakistan together by turning flame-throwers machine-guns hand-grenades on the city slums . . . take turns in vomitting as their nostrils are assailed by the stench of burning slums (426-27)

Finally incapable of continuing in the submissive performance of his duty, Saleem took to his heels and fled. It appeared as if an "overdose of reality gave birth to a miasmic longing for flight into the safety of dreams." (431)

The degrading identity of a sniffer dog marks in one way the nadir of Saleem's quest for identity. Paradoxically it also paves the way to reconstruction of his life.

Saleem's drift into the Sundarbans along with the three soldiers symbolises the total loss of identity. He is lost in a jungle so thick that history never found its way in. In the Sundarbans the four men succumb to the logic of the jungle, then acquire the skills of survival, gradually evolve into a new adulthood and peace and rest at a Hindu temple. From this easeful time Saleem wakes up, as Mario Couto says, "like a latter day Odysseus tearing himself from the arms of Calypso who both soothes his pain and robs him of the challenge of achievement."[8] They realised that the temple was fooling them into using up their dreams by giving them their hearts' desire. Saleem now views the temple with new eyes and tears himself from the forest of illusions. In the Sundarbans it is once again snake poison that helps him to regain his memory. Out of the Sundarbans, Saleem is in a daze when he sees the human waste created by war. In a series of bizarre incidents he loses his companions. A lonely and forlorn Saleem wanders the streets of Dhaka, still unable to recall his name. He becomes aware of his name through Parvati, another midnight child, who has come along with a band of magicians to celebrate the Indian victory over Pakistan and to participate in the creation of a new nation Bangladesh. Through her, he not only recovers his name but is also smuggled to India in her magic basket. As he pops out of the basket in India he wants to bury the identity of his past and wants to embark on a new life, and to choose his own undestined future.

From this moment onwards Saleem embarks on a process of reconstruction. His search for identity now on his own terms unfolds. After a short stay in the magicians' ghetto, Saleem in his quest for identity shifts to his uncle Mustafa's house. He has visions of embarking on a nation-saving mission through his bureaucrat uncle. Ironically what he does realise a little late is that his uncle himself does not have an identity either in his own home or in his official life. Disillusioned once again, he goes back to the magicians' ghetto. Saleem now hopes to embark on one last mission of direct communication with the masses with the help of Picture Singh, a snake charmer and his last father figure. The emergency imposed by the widow drives the last nail into Saleem's ambitious vision. Saleem is taken to the widow's hostel where he is forced to reveal the identities of the other midnight children. Citing them as a threat to her over vaulting ambition, she has all the midnight children vasectomised. Now drained of all hope, Saleem in the widow's hostel ruminates on the nature of politics. He comes to the conclusion that "politics at the best of times is a dirty business" (518), hence to be avoided. He feels that he shouldn't have dreamt of purpose at all since "privacy in the small individual lives of men was preferable to all the inflated macrocosmic activity." (518) Saleem, at the end of it all, is highly critical of the modern state when he says that the midnight children were just "the grotesque aberrational monsters of Independence" and as a result the "modern nation state could have neither time nor compassion." (517)

Saleem's retrieval from the anonymity of being the buddha in the Sundarbans and the hopes of a purposeful and meaningful life is sadly negated by the emergency. The new leaders who took over from Indira Gandhi did not represent a new dawn. To Saleem it seemed obscene that the atrocities committed by the emergency on human dignity was soon forgotten due to the burdens of daily life. Saleem is confident that his son Aadam Sinai, emergency's child, is more determined and does not easily give to dreams.

Saleem's search for identity is sometimes grimly factual and sometimes lapsing into dreams. Though his attempts at creating history are thwarted, he is not disappointed. The novel surely does not end on a pessimistic note, as it is generally believed. Replying to the question on the pessimistic end, in an interview Rushdie says:

> I don't think that the end of the book suggests a negative view. Saleem's personal destiny does lead to despair, but Saleem does not represent the whole of India, but only one historical process, a certain kind of hope that is lost and which exhausts itself with the death of Saleem. But in the way the book is written I am suggesting also reserves beyond this the multitudinous possibilities that India generates. I think I have shown that although the possibility that Saleem represents is finished, a new and tougher generation is just ahead.[9]

Commenting on the ending of the novel, Ron Blabber says, "For Saleem the promise and hope associated with the 'mythic' midnight children will always fall victim to the history of the times. But the despair is not total; buried within the process is hope that the cycle will be broken."[10] The hope that the tougher generation of Aadam Sinai might succeed in their quest is not too far-fetched and a consoling thought.

II

In *Midnight's Children*, Saleem Sinai, the hero is at the outset confident about his centrality in the scheme of things. However, by the time the story ends, he is pushed to the periphery, becomes marginalised. All his attempts at finding purpose and identity steadily push him from his illusory centrality to the periphery. On the other hand, in *Shame* Omar Khayyam Shakil is presented as a peripheral hero at the beginning. Hence his search for identity basically involves an attempt to get into the mainstream of life. His search may not be as spectacular as that of Saleem Sinai but is nothing in terms of intensity.

Comparing the two novels Timothy Hyman comments, "*Shame* stands to *Midnight's Children* very much as Pakistan to India, a smaller book for a meaner world."[11] The narrative on the personal level begins with the mysterious birth of Omar Khayyam Shakil. He is raised under bizarre circumstances by the three sisters in that equally bizarre mansion, "Nishapur" which symbolises an area of darkness, intrigue and anonymity.

While the public plot focuses primarily on the political rivalries, the private lives of the women are equally important and, as the author intervenes to inform us, "Refract" or perhaps even "Subsume the male plot." (173) M.D. Fletcher succinctly sums up the interaction of the plots:

> The various plots are integrated in circular fashion into one story from Omar through Isky and Raza to the wives and daughters to Sufiya and back to Omar with Sufia also cut-

> ting across the diameter of the circle to complete the violent destruction of the male sphere in the end.[12]

The plot has all the seeming trappings of a tragedy, but is not really so, for as Rushdie explains "The work combines a plot comprised of the stuff of tragedy but with a cast of gangsters, clowns, hoodlums, necessitating that it be written like a farce, a kind of macabre black farce."[13]

Saleem Sinai in *Midnight's Children* is bedevilled by a dual perception of reality as it exists in India and Pakistan. His experience of the multi-dimensional reality of India clashes with the uni-dimensional ordered reality of Pakistan. Omar Khayyam Shakil on the other hand is not exposed to such confusing duality of perception, for his experience is only limited to the latter. From his birth his destiny is anonymous, divorced from the national history, while Saleem Sinai is inextricably linked to history of the nation.

Omar Khayyam Shakil starts life with a distinct disadvantage. He is conceived and raised under bizarre by the three Shakil sisters. Secluded from the world by an eccentric father strictly abiding by the rules of purdah, the three sisters break out with a vengeance after their father's death. This results in the birth of a child who is, as Griffin A. Chausse says, "the standard bearer and personification of their misguided legacy."[14] The conception of Omar Khayyam Shakil with the identity of both father and mother left deliberately undefined, is their gesture of revolt against their earlier cloistered and unhealthy existence. Michael Hollington aptly observes, "His ontological insecurity is in some measure the product of the secrecy and mystery that surround the circumstances of his paternity and maternity."[15] Omar Khayyam Shakil passes twelve long years, the most crucial years of development, trapped inside that reclusive mansion, described by Afzal Khan Fawzia as "a sort of concentrated decrepitude made up of decomposing remnants discarded ideas and forgotten dreams."[16] For twelve long years Omar Khayyam views the outer world through his telescope, spying out of the upper storey window, since those on the ground floor were permanently shut-tered. The fleeting glimpses of the vibrant outside world serves as a contrast to the stagnant gloomy world of Nishapur. The only other link with the outside world is provided by the dumb-waiter. His seemingly idle exploration of Nishapur is ironically not completely useless, as it yields him a book case "stuffed with the volumes of the theory and practice of hypnosis," (33) which leads him to a "lifelong involvement with that arcane science which has so awesome a power for good or ill." (34) The knowledge garnered from these books, practised successfully on the maid Hasmat bibi and on his classmate Farah Zoraster, provides the base for later experiences, both good and evil. It gives him the means of debauchery in the company of Isky Harappa and later, provides him with a chance to redeem himself through his treatment of Sufiya Zinobia.

Rushdie concretises the impact of this unnatural upbringing on a child of superior perceptions in his over whimsical manner. Shakil's distorted vision of the world, which persists throughout the novel, has its origins in the moments after his birth, when the baby is held upside down. An extension of this infantile inversion in Shakil's increasing sense of imbalance, "He was afflicted from his earlier days, by a sense of inversion, of a world turned upside down. And by something worse—the fear that he was living at the edge of the world." (21) The vertigo with which he is afflicted is a symbolic manifestation of a sense of disorientation which eternally troubles him. The narrator intervenes to reiterate the significance of this recurring problem of his peripheral hero:

> Hell above, paradise below, I have lingered on this account of Omar Khayyam's original, unstable wilderness to underline the propositions that he grew up between twin eternities, whose conventional order was, in his experience precisely inverted. (23)

It is not merely the physical confines of Nishapur that is claustrophobic to the growing child, even more suffocating is the unhealthy relationship existing among his mothers as well as between them and himself. The three women are portrayed as close minded, dictatorial and repressive. He watches them for a dozen years and hates them "for their closeness, their three-in-oneness which redoubled that sense of exclusion, of being in the midst of objects, out of things." (35) Omar Khayyam gradually realises that his apparent freedom in the house is merely "pseudo-liberty of a zoo animal, and his mothers were his loving caring keepers." (35) The fragmented nature of the relationship implants in him the conviction of being a peripheral personality, a watcher from the wings of his own life. The attitudes of the mothers, the symbolic shutting of the doors of Nishapur, the archaeological antiquity of Nishapur with its crumbling walls and out-dated Neolithic pottery all coalesce to create a world entombed in the past. The ignorance about his father's identity troubles him endlessly and to confound it all is an equally disturbing uncertainty about who among the three sisters is his real mother. All these contribute to a sense of imbalance, confusion of identity, a disturbing feeling of peripheral leading to increasing restlessness and a strong desire to break free from these shackles.

On his twelfth birthday, Omar Khayyam makes his first gesture of independence when he demands to be sent to school. Contrary to his expectations, the changes are merely superficial and lack substance. The old problems continue to haunt him. He realises that narrowness of outlook is not limited to his mothers in Nishapur but extends to people like Maulana Dawood and the postman who are equally narrow minded in a wide world. He makes a determined effort to trace his father and failing, takes recourse to father figures like Eduardo Rodrigues, his schoolmaster. The idea that he has broken free from the past is merely an illusion and this is clearly indicated by his delight in voyeurism. His voyeurism reveals to him the hitherto, unknown rich and cryptic texture of human life. What he fails to realise is that this too can give only substitute gratification, that he is savouring life through other human beings and thus continues to be on the peripheries of life. It is the schoolmaster-father figure who recognizes the true peripheral nature of the boy, his inclination to confine himself to the sidelines of life. Rodrigues attempts to push his protege from the peripheries to the centre, "To succeed in life," he told the boy, "One must be of the essence yes, make yourself essential, that's the ticket . . . be a doctor . . . what's a doctor after all? A legitimised voyeur, a stranger yet also paradoxically, central, especially at the crisis." (49) And at a later stage he does exactly that, when he secures a medical scholarship in Karachi, carrying the legacy of his mothers' strange advice when he had first stepped outside the crumbling portals of Nishapur. Wishing to armour him against the expected hostility of the outside world directed against his shameful origins, they had instructed him to sacrifice not just shame "but also embarrassment, discomfiture, decency, modesty, shyness, the sense of having an ordained place in the world." (39) The author significantly intervenes to emphasise the lasting impact of this advice on Omar Khayyam Shakil, "Can it be doubted that Omar Khayyam having been barred from feeling shame at an early age, continued to be affected by that remarkable ban throughout his later years, years yes, after his escape from his mothers' zone of influence." (39) His odyssey has just begun.

Burdened with this kind of unhealthy advice, it is inevitable that his search for identity takes a wrong direction, manifesting itself in a negative form. When he re-enters the narrative at the age of thirty-five, he has earned a high reputation as a doctor and an equally low reputation as human being, in Sushila Singh's words "a degenerate without shame."[17] Through Rani Humayun and Biliquis Hyder we catch fleeting glimpses of a man who is not only a debauch himself but leads others on to similar excesses. As Biliquis maliciously informs Rani, "Who hasn't seen your Isky and that doctor run around belly dancer shows, international hotel swimming pools . . . that Shakil fixes everything like a pimp or what . . . the two of them go to the red light area with movie cameras." (93) The utter disgust of the entire city at his uncouth behaviour is given expression by Rani when she says, "Fellow doesn't know the meaning of the word [shame]; as if some essential part of his education has been overlooked or perhaps he has deliberately chosen to expunge the word from his vocabulary lest it's explosive." (81) Omar Khayyam Shakil's moral degeneration finds a powerful physical manifestation in his increasingly disproportionate physical contours. The enormity of his inner shamelessness is directly proportional to the enormity of his physical bulk. The narrative deliberately links the two when Rani remarks on the occasion of his appearance at her wedding to Isky Harappa, "Quiet a shameless fellow to carry all that tummy and fat about and all." (80)

In this stage of the quest for identity Omar Khayyam begins to assert influence, but because of the distortions of his personality, the influence is wholly negative. The full impact of this negative influence is seen through two inter related incidents. On the first occasion at a party, he is witness to both Isky and Raza's attempts to win the favours of the beautiful Pinky Aurangezeb, culminating in the suave Isky walking away triumphantly with his prize; "Watching from the sidelines was the flabby Himalayan figure of our peripheral hero, the doctor Omar Khayyam Shakil." (106) On a second occasion, at a party in Mohenjo, a drunken Omar Khayyam rouses the ire of Biliquis and her husband Raza against Isky Harappa, indicating that they had been dishonoured by the latter. This provokes Raza into frenzied anger and an insane wish to challenge Isky to duel unto death. Although this volatile situation is diffused, the fire of discord has been irreparably fanned by Omar Khayyam's thoughtless interference. This fire of discord has vital bearing on the unfolding national drama, as it brings the principal protagonists on the path of confrontation.

Paradoxically, it is Isky Harappa's unceremonious rejection of Omar Khayyam that reiterates the peripheral nature of his identity. His association with Isky Harappa has given him some sort of acceptability in society; "Some of Isky's saratorical ways have rubbed off on him . . . he carries a present from his friend Iskander; a silver-headed sword stick from the Ansu valley, twelve inches of polished steel concealed in intricately-carved walnut." (127) However, the fear of falling off the edge of the world troubles him every now and then. At such times when he is assailed by the old vertigo, "he leans heavily on his sword concealing cane to prevent himself from falling." (126) His dependence on the silver headed cane symbolises his relationship with Isky, through which he has gained, temporarily at least, a sense of identity. When Isky develops a new interest in politics, he realises the necessity of changing his way of life. Pinky Aurangzeb and Omar Khayyam are summarily obliterated from his life. Isky even instructs his gatekeeper, "When that degenerate comes to call, just throw the badmash on his fat bottom and watch him bounce." (125) Realising that he no longer has the symbolic stick to lean on, the sad truth of his peripheral identity is brought home to him with a renewed and severe attack of vertigo; "So severe at Isky's rejection that he fell sick at the back of the taxi." (126) It requires of Omar Khayyam Shakil to find an identity now on his own terms.

The third and final stage of his quest begins with an apparent similarity to the preceding one but soon transforms its nature. "Ditched by one great figure of the period, Omar Khayyam seeks to hitch himself to another star." (144) But it is this relationship which offers the chance to redeem himself and finally procures an identity for the peripheral hero. The most monumental encounter of his life occurs when he is called in to treat the psychosomatic disorder of Sufiya Zinobia, the mentally retarded daughter of Raza Hyder. She is by far the most intriguing character of the novel, rich with symbolic overtones. Sufiya's psychosomatic disorders accompanied by occasional outbursts of terrible violence, are symbolic of the ills that plague the nation and the inevitable outburst which will follow. As Michael Hollington comments on the role of Sufiya, "Sufiya can be said to stand for the necessary violent reaction, of the women against patriarchy and of the people against dictatorship."[18] She is projected as the embodiment of "shame" and is disparagingly referred to as such by her mother. The parents' sense of shame at their inability to fulfill the expectations of their society by bearing a male child is tragically imposed on the hapless child. She is the product of misconstrued notions of shame which flourish in a society which is inhumanly rigid in its norms.

Most critics have limited their understanding of Omar

Khayyam Shakil by seeing him only in terms of shamelessness till the very end. On the contrary there is a well-defined movement away from shamelessness after his association with Sufiya Zenobia. When Sufiya enters Omar Khayyam's life, twelve years of unloved humiliation have already taken their toll. Omar Khayyam's instantaneous love for her is totally uncharacteristic of a man who has not thought beyond himself. Both are born outside the misconceived norms of society and they share an affinity as marginalised people. Hence it is logical in the scheme of things that these two people—one representing shame, the other shamelessness should be united. D.B. Jewison remarks: "The narrator seems to be suggesting that in such a consummation the polarities would mingle and free humanity from its curse."[19] In short Omar Khayyam Shakil "had fallen for his destiny." (141) These two discordant people, a twelve-year-old retarded beauty and fifty-year-old man with a dubious past, are united in the physical and social marital ties. Omar Khayyam's first acquaintance with Sufiya's capacity for horrifying violence is during the marriage of her younger sister Naveed Hyder to Talvar-Ul-Haq. A painful distinction has been maintained from birth between the two sisters, the distinction concretised by one being called "Shame" and the other "Goodnews" by their mother. Her repressed, perhaps even unconscious anger at the injustice of this discrimination bursts out in full fury when she sees her sister enjoying what had been denied to her. In an act of barbaric violence she almost wrenches Talvar-Ul-Haq's head off during the marriage. Omar Khayyam had witnessed this alarming transformation and had used his hypnotic skill more than he had ever done before to bring Sufiya out of her self-induced trance. The long hinted at nikah between Sufiya and Omar Khayyam takes place. The marriage not only provides him with the scope of becoming the confidant, of another man, moulding the fate of the nation, it also provides him an opportunity to redefine himself as a human being through his tender care of Sufiya. His physical transformation keeps pace with the more important internal changes. His physical girth had remarkably diminished to almost normal dimensions. He develops a hitherto unknown respect for himself and views himself with new eyes, "I may be no movie star, he told his mirror, but I have ceased to be a cartoon." (211) The transformation prompts the Parsee ayah to comment, "You're not such a wreck as you say." (212) It is a long way from Rani Harappa's earlier comment about him. The man who had in his earlier days abandoned Farah Zoraster to face an unwanted pregnancy alone, now shows an increasing sense of responsibility in his concern for Shahbanu, a mere ayah.

This human concern finds its full expression in his loving care of his retarded wife. The image of Sufiya begins to merge with that of a nation increasingly repressed with the religious fanaticism of Raza Hyder. Her increasing bouts of violence symbolically reflect the mood of a long-suffering nation. Raza too seems to have made this identification and thinks that in silencing Sufiya he would be able to regain control over the nation. What had started in Pinky Aurangzeb's backyard had now spread to the whole nation. This had elevated Sufiya to the status of a terrifying myth. Pushed against the wall, Raza confides in Omar the necessity of eliminating Sufiya through a "fatal injection." At that moment Omar shows great courage and compassion in refusing to heed Hyder and insists on treatment through hypnosis and his expertise. This is the turning point in Omar Khayyam's life. And as the narrator comments "Courage is a rarer thing than evil after all." (235) M.D. Fletcher observes: "It is at this stage that Omar's general nature seems to change, when he refuses to kill Sufiya with a painless injection despite the danger posed by her increasing violent symptoms."[20] As an unavoidable part of the treatment, Sufiya is chained in a secret cellar and kept constantly drugged, transformed from a beast to a sleeping beauty. In spite of Omar's constant and tender watch, one night she makes good her escape. Significantly, this happens on the day Isky Harappa is unjustly hanged, an act of ultimate shame of a repressive leader. Sufiya's escape symbolically represents a nation breaking free from its repressive shackles.

After many trials and tribulations, the trio of Omar Shakil, Raza Hyder and Biliquis arrive in the town of Q, ironically sheltered by the "Burqua." Thus Omar Khayyam's quest for identity comes full circle with the return to Nishapur. Nemesis awaits these two men in the crumbling mansion. Haunted by the premonition of death fed on rumours of Sufiya's ominous approach towards Q, Omar Khayyam bursts out in rancour:

> I am a peripheral man. Other persons have been the principal actors in my story. Hyder and Harappa my leading men. . . . I watched from the wings, not knowing how to act. I confess to social climbing, to only-doing-my-job, to being corner man in other people's wrestling matches. (283)

Ironically it is this assertion and realisation of his peripheral nature which confirms how far he has moved from the peripheries. Paradoxically it is an indication that he has been able to rise beyond these infirmities and forge a more positive identity for himself. Unlike Raza Hyder Omar Khayyam is terrified neither of Sufiya's spectral presence nor of the prospect of death. Raza Hyder who is terrified of the imminent confrontation with Sufiya, is virtually a dead man, even before his gruesome death in the dumb-waiter engineered by the three vindictive mothers of Omar Khayyam. On the contrary, Omar Khayyam faces Sufiya and death with equanimity, confident of the knowledge that in his own unheroic way, his quest for identity has been fulfilled. The novel ends with a violent explosion, reducing Nishapur to smithereens. Paul Sharrad comments, "Like Sufiya Zinobia's somnambulist outrages, the novel is an outburst exposing the shame of others before it becomes demonic through prolonged repression. It is also born of the writer's 'blushing' for the shame of the world and of himself as a displaced person."[21] The gesture of farewell from its unprepossessing hero is a confirmation of his changed status. Positive human values have not only been the redemption of Omar Khayyam the individual; it indicates the path of redemption of a repressed nation.

III

Amitav Ghosh's first novel *The Circle of Reason* is a bee-hive of activity. Characters flit in and out like actors on a Shakespearean stage or as in Chaucer's Canterbury tales, each with his own story, told in a flavour and style which is his own.

The novel lends itself to interpretation at two levels. On the surface, according to S. Sengupta, *The Circle of Reason* might give the impression that it is a picaresque novel set in the contemporary milieu. It does have an unheroic hero and records various adventures befalling him and his inter-action with a host of other characters as he moves from one country to another.[22] The movement from one country to another is not merely a narrative device to widen the scope of the novel. It is used to underline a very important aspect of human life. It can be best understood in the words of James Clifford when he says, "Ghosh's work . . . underlines the novelist's interest in travelling as a metaphor for the human condition."[23] This briskly paced narrative, at a deeper level, explores the struggle between the power of cold heartless reason and the nurturing power of human qualities which follow no rules yet bring a healing touch to all mankind.

The protagonist Alu's search for identity unfolds against this background. A passionate commitment to a goal tempered by human touch forms the focus of Alu's quest for identity. With this idea in perspective, Alu's quest passes through three distinct stages. His odyssey starts in Lalpukur, a small border village in Bengal. The second stage unfolds itself in al-Ghazira, a fictitious country in the Middle East, the new oil rich town with its fascinating mix of fortune hunters from various countries. At both these stages Alu's attempts to seek an identity ends disastrously. And as the narrative reaches its denouement in El Oued, the Algerian Sahara, the third stage of Alu's quest takes a decisive and positive turn which puts him on the right path to self-discovery and hope.

Orphaned at the age of eight, Nachiketa comes to live with his uncle Balaram Bose in Lalpukur. And there he is renamed

Alu by Bolai-da due to the shape of his head "curiously uneven, bulging all over with knots and bumps." (9) Incidentally this grotesque appearance links Alu with the protagonists of Rushdie's novels—a clear indication that the protagonists of the novel of the Eighties have moved away from the prototype of the romantic hero. In Lalpukur, Alu is wedged between an uncle obsessed with phrenology and an aunt equally with the sewing machine. Apparently discordant in their natures—one an intellectual rationalist, the other superstitious and tradition bound, they are paradoxically similar in the manner in which their respective obsessions reduce them both to irrationality. In this stage of the quest for identity Alu is merely an observer, but his sensitive and receptive mind unconsciously absorbs signals transmitted by his exposure to people like his aunt and uncle.

Alu's Uncle, Balaram Bose prides himself on his rationality. He passionately believes that phrenology is a rational science based on the belief that, "the inside and the outside, the head and the body, what people do and what they are, are one." (14) Armed with this belief, he moves around with his contraption called the claws, making predictions based on shapes of peoples' heads. The superficiality of Balaram's knowledge of a dubious science is seen in his constantly changing assessments of Alu's nature and future. Balaram initially felt that:

> A witches' brew could be bubbling in that lump of a head—destructiveness perhaps, mixed with Amativeness or secrecy and peppered with combativeness or Acquisitiveness. And if one could find no way of identifying and combating those organs it would be just a matter of time before they drove the boy to some hideous crime. (9)

He changed his opinion when he felt that "it avoided destructiveness and secretiveness and Acquisitiveness." (10) The obsession takes a dangerous turn when Balaram Bose is requested to predict the future of Bhudeb Roy's infant son. His pronouncements only help to widen the rift between them, and put them on the direct path of confrontation. With an utter disregard to the sentiments of a parent, Balaram Bose had pronounced that the infant child had typical homicidal tendencies. The trouble with Bhudeb Roy led his wife Toru Debi to insist on his abandoning his study of Phrenology, which is temporarily revived with Alu's coming to Lalpukur. A more dangerous obsession is with the idea of cleanliness, the instrument of which is carbolic acid. It originates when war refugees stream into the border village of Lalpukur. Oblivious to the human tragedy behind the refugee influx, blinded by an overwhelming preoccupation with cleanliness, Balaram Bose plunges onto the task of cleaning the refugee shanties with carbolic acid.

Alu by nature is a quiet child. it takes him some time to adjust to his new surroundings. Like another isolated child Omar Khayyam Shakil, Alu too is a voracious reader, devouring the books in Balaram's library with passionate interest. Unfortunately Bhudeb Roy's sons hound him out from school. Disturbed by his orphaned nephew's impassivity and lack of emotion, Balaram Bose had attempted to reach out to the boy. Urging him to "forget the past and look to the future" he reassured him "that one could do anything with the future, one could change the world." (28) He advocates the idea "that to change the world one needs to have passion" (28) and quotes the instance of Louis Pasteur's courageous convictions that changed the course of history. This strikes a chord in the consciousness of the sensitive boy, and for the first time he displays emotion. His frequent visits to Shombu Debnath, the enigmatic weaver, lead his uncle to suspect that he is interested in weaving. Balaram's phrenological studies of Alu's physical appearance confirm his surmise. "His intuition was proved in every detail; Alu's body, his hands, his legs, his arms, not to speak of the organ, corresponded exactly to his calculation of the proportions ideal for a weaver." (55) To his great joy Alu is apprenticed to Shombu Debnath. Moving from weaving coarse cloth to the finest Jamdani, the young Alu seems well on the way to creating a pattern in his life. This tragically disrupted when he is caught in the vortex of the turbulent passions of Bhudeb Roy, his uncle and aunt. After discarding phrenology, Balaram Bose had taken equally passionately to the idea of cleanliness. As war breaks out and refugees stream into Lalpukur, Balaram takes up passionately the task of cleaning up the refugee shanties with carbolic acid. As Bolai-da wryly comments, "This is a new Balaram babu. It was true; Balaram, antiseptic and pungent with disinfectant, had never been so happy." (61) His excessive irrational obsession with cleanliness had made him oblivious to the human tragedy surrounding him. A similar weakness earlier proved dangerous during his forays into phrenology. This new passionate devotion leads him to a blunder whose consequences are tragic. Paranoid about germs, he begins to see Bhudeb Roy too as the most dangerous germ of them all. He incites Shombu Debnath to pour carbolic acid on Bhudeb Roy's head when he is addressing a political meeting. The simmering animosity between the two men now erupts into open conflict and results in outright violence, compounded by Bhudeb Roy's suspicion that Balaram Bose had abetted in Shombu Debnath's elopement with his wife.

Alu is a witness and participant in Balaram Bose's growing fanaticism. He is also witness to Balaram's School of Reason, its initial euphoria and its gradual descent into obscurity. Balaram Bose's School of Reason, according to Robert Dixon, "alternatively bores and terrorises people with his scientific notions, and eventually destroys the village by sterilizing the village carbolic acid."[24] When his uncle runs out of money to replenish his stock of carbolic acid, Alu supports him financially. Inspired by his uncle's insistence that passion is the only way to changing the world, Alu sees it in action in his uncle's obsession. He is also a mute witness to how destructive passion can be in reality. A passion for politics and the love of money are Bhudeb Roy's obsessions. He regards Balaram Bose as the greatest obstacle in his path to fame and wealth. Circumstances play into Bhudeb Roy's hands, when Shombu Debnath's son Rakhal stores crude home made bombs for sale to the extremists in Balaram's house. This provides Bhudeb Roy with the long awaited opportunity of hitting back at both his opponents. Accusing them of being extremists, he summons the police to conduct a raid on Balaram's house. In a bizarre accident, a flare sent up by the police as a warning falls on the house stocked with carbolic acid and bombs reducing the house to smithreens. Surrounded by danger, Toru-Debi feels that she has been abandoned by her singular passion, the sewing machine, when it suddenly stops working, she stood up and put the sewing machine in Alu's arms, "Throw it into the pond, she said, It's dead." (47) This providentially saves Alu's life. Now branded an extremist, Alu is forced to leave Lalpukur. The first stage of his quest for identity has seen him as an observer of passions of various kinds. In the next stage, the realisation becomes more conscious as he becomes the principal actor of his own story.

Hunted down as an extremist, with the policeman Jyoti Das hot on his heels, Alu moves from place to place in search of safety. In Calcutta his uncle's friend Gopal provides him shelter. A chance encounter with Rajan, a mill worker, provides Alu with the means of evading an unjustified arrest:

> He passed down a chain of Rajan's Chalia kinsmen, scattered over every factory along the South-Eastern railway, paying out parts of his eight thousand rupees where Rajan had told him to, down, steadily southwards stooping to catch his breath in the great mills of Madurai and Coimbatore, till whispers came that the police had orders and a sketch, Rajan had been taken in—then it was time to leave the railways behind, time to slip into the forests of the Nilgiris—then over the water-sheds into Kerala—he spent the nights secreted away in the Chalia quarters of scattered villages—but then again suddenly rumours of informers of reports to the police, so faster still westwards, down through the mountains, faster and faster. (157)

Cast adrift without a house or an identity, the pattern of his life disrupted by forces beyond his control, Alu finds himself in a boat as dilapidated as his own condition. The boat "Mariamma" is on its way to al-Ghazira, carrying a load of fortune hunters. As Fakrul Alam comments, "Illegal immigrants they hazard their lives by voyaging on frail vessels."[25] The turbulent sea voyage sees the beginning of a meaningful association with Zindi. Zindi, a middle-aged woman running an establishment for illegal migrants in al-Ghazira, perhaps senses the boy's plight and takes him under her protective care. An embodiment of practicality, she is also capable of sporadic displays of compassion. "I will give you a chance because you are helpful kind of turd—I'll give you a place and I'll find you work aren't easy to get." (181) Zindi's patronising benevolence helps Alu to re-establish a certain rhythm in his life, but one which is still dictated by others. Six months of this uneventful and monotonous life is broken when Alu is buried under thousands and thousands of tons of concrete of an immense building called Al-Najma, the Star. In an ironical co-incidence he is once again saved by two old sewing machines which hold up a gigantic girder. Alu's original name Nachiketa has a special significance at this moment. In the Upanishads, Nachiketa is the name of the boy who obeying his father waits at Yama's door. When Yama grants him a boon, Nachiketa goes for the ultimate knowledge—the secret of life and death. The name's significance becomes apparent when Alu is buried under the Star and given up for dead. Nachiketa/Alu is at death's door for four days refusing food and water, but all the time in deep contemplation. As Alu's friends go inside the ruins of the Star, Robert Dixon comments, "they find themselves lost in the postmodern space of collapsed glass and concrete doom."[26] It recalls Saleem Sinai's experience in *Midnight's Children* when he is lost in the Sundarbans. Unlike the mythological Nachiketa, his quest is not for knowledge of the universe, the infinitely large, but about "cleanliness and infinitely small." (235) In the words of G.J.V. Prasad, his quest "is not for the understanding of the life after but for knowledge of the cause of the ills of society, the life present."[27] This once again reiterates that in the Indian English novel of the Eighties, the quest for identity is in the terms of the concrete socio-political realities of contemporary existence.

His miraculous escape creates a mystical aura about Alu and elevates him to a semi-Messiah status. The quest for identity appears to be taking a definite form as, for the first time, Alu finds himself on the centre-stage of his life. When he comes back the people of the Ras are eager to hear his words of wisdom, and he holds forth on "the germ." He declares that the enemy of mankind is money, "which travels on every man and on every woman, silently preparing for their defeat, turning one against the other." (281) The conscious use of the word "germ" establishes a correspondence between the passion of Alu and that of his uncle. This helps to anticipate the disastrous consequences of Alu's newfound passion.

The transformation that he undergoes while buried in the debris is almost taken to the realms of fantasy. A subdued, withdrawn teenager, with no indication of a special calling, is miraculously transformed temporarily into a Messiah. Once again, this is reminiscent of Saleem Sinai who gets his moment of enlightenment while lying hidden in the washing chest. The people of the Ras are intrigued by Alu's refusal of food or water and his insistence of being left alone to think. When Alu finally emerges unscathed, they are eager to hear his words of wisdom. During the phase of reflection, hitherto disjointed elements of his past come together to produce Alu's theory of the real germ of mankind. His uncle's passionate devotion to cleanliness, inspired by Pasteur's battle against germs perhaps combined with subconscious loathing of the money power of Bhudeb Roy finds expression in Alu's analysis of money being the greatest scourge of mankind. He felt that Louis Pasteur's experiment with germs was incomplete because he had dealt with only physical germs, Alu's perceptions were broader. Perhaps taken aback by his sudden elevation to the position of spiritual authority, Alu withdraws into silence and detachment, taking up weaving as an attempt once again to weave a realistic pattern of his life, leaving others to put his theories into practice. His enigmatic message delivered, Alu once again reverts to the role of observer, leaving others to enact a farcical drama. Inspired by his new found beliefs, the old mildness vanishes. An impressive aura now surrounds him, he "sat with his hands folded on his lap, absolutely still, but his voice grew in strength and power until it reached the courtyard and into the lanes and gullies outside." (280)

The basis of an egalitarian society seems to be laid by Prof. Samuel's plan of a common pool of earnings, aimed to reduce the workers' attachment to money. Ironically, the plan boomerangs for it leads to increased material prosperity which in turn, increases man's avarice. A shopping expedition by the people of the Ras is tragically misinterpreted by the new rulers of al-Ghazira. In a drastic measure to curb what they interpret as labour unrest, the regime unleashes a violent attack on the migrant workers, killing and wounding some, and dislocating many. Once again, Alu has a providential escape. Once again his attempts to live a meaningful existence, to search for an identity is brutally aborted. He finds himself once again adrift and homeless. However this time he has the support of Zindi and Kulfi, a young woman with whom he has established an undefined yet obviously intimate relationship.

There is a distinct parallelism between the first and the second stages of Alu's quest for identity. In the former, Balaram's basic obsession with cleanliness precipitated the disaster. In the latter, it is Alu's passion for a different kind of cleanliness which results in disaster. In both cases it is evident that passions become dangerous when they ignore the reality of human nature and existence. This similarity is clearly reinforced through the motif of carbolic acid. In the first section, carbolic acid is used to cleanse the power and money hungry Bhudeb Roy. Similarly it is used in the second section, to cleanse the biggest germs of al-Ghazira, the business establishments and the Muggadams.

In the first section he had been a passive victim of his unrealistic passions, whereas in the second he is directly responsible for his predicament, the loss of direction and balance in his quest for identity.

Weaving has been the predominant symbol throughout Amitav Ghosh's work. His Ph.D. thesis at Oxford was on the history of weaving and the cloth trade between Britain and India in the 19th century. In *The Circle of Reason* weaving is a recurrent symbol which functions at various levels. In the context of the protagonist's search for identity it clearly stands for the evolution of a pattern of living. Alu who had taken up weaving after his miraculous survival suddenly finds himself with atrophied thumbs on his way to El-Oued. His atrophied thumbs are a physical manifestation of his inner mental paralysis. It seems as if his search for identity has reached a state of stasis.

The third and the most decisive part of Alu's quest unfolds itself in El-Oued. Even as the denouement of the plot is placed in the little town of El-Oued, Alu's life too embarks on a new beginning. For the first time Alu comes across a complete person in his life. The fugitive party comprising of Alu, Zindi, Kulfi and the sick child Boss can hardly believe their luck when they see an Indian woman walking down the road. She too is equally surprised to see them and gives them shelter.

The Indian woman Mrs. Verma, a brisk and no-nonsensical doctor, takes the new arrivals under her wing and persuades them to participate in the staging of the dance drama 'Chitrangada.' More importantly she manages to disabuse Alu of the dream of a world purified by rational methods. As Kulfi dies at the climax of the rehearsal of 'Chitrangada,' Mrs. Verma's personality, a fine balance between reason and spirit comes out forcefully. The compassionate Mrs. Verma struggles with adverse circumstances to arrange a traditional Indian funeral for her in the middle of the Sahara. In spite of the vehement protests of Dr. Mishra, what she says forms the crux of her character:

> Rules, rules, she said softly. All you ever talk about is rules. That's how you and your kind have destroyed everything—science, religion, socialism—with your rules and orthodoxies. That's the difference between us: you worry about rules and I worry about being human. (409)

In other words Mrs. Verma makes a passionate plea for reaffirmation of the basic qualities of the heart. As Mrs. Verma points out when she is trying to go through the rituals before the burial:

> What does it matter whether it's Gangajal to be used for cleaning the place or carbolic acid? It's just a question of cleaning the place, isn't it? People thought something was

> clean once, now they think something else is clean. What difference does it make to the dead? (411)

Mrs. Verma's sincere efforts have a tremendous effect on Alu's sensibilities, particularly in contrast to the callous manner in which Zindi had been rejected by the very relatives who owed their prosperity to her. Instead of theorising, Alu learns to participate in life, when he chops wood for the funeral of his "wife" Kulfi. When it comes to lighting the funeral pyre, he realises that his thumbs have become normal, which in its atrophied condition earlier had troubled him a great deal. Mrs. Verma's words are significant when she says, "It is a little muscular atrophy but you can do whatever you like as long as you want to." (417) A rejuvenated Alu emerges from the depths of despair. It is significant that this occurs immediately after they have consigned the *Life of Pasteur* to the funeral pyre, suggesting that pure reason cannot take man very far on the path of human compassion. But the death of reason is not a pessimistic view of life as Mrs. Verma points out: "If there's one thing people learn from the past, it is that every consummated death is another beginning." (414) The most important thing to learn is to "make do with what we've got, and in the meantime try to be a better human being." (414) The book *Life of Pasteur* the original culprit which is crucial to the narrative starts in the first part and makes its way through the middle parts and is finally and symbolically consigned to the flames in the last part. The novel drives home the point that reason will remain incomplete without the touch of human emotion. On a larger scale the author/text seems to be saying that the crux of the socio-political imbroglio of this country is precisely due to the gap between passionate commitment and human touch.

Thus disburdened of false dreams, a new Alu is waiting to go back home. For Alu, life has come a full circle as he settles down to wait for Virat Singh and the ship that would carry him home. For Alu hope is the beginning. And now it is not too far-fetched to visualise a new Alu at the loom harmoniously weaving a pattern of his life in the time to come.

IV

Amitav Ghosh's second novel *The Shadow Lines* at the outset establishes a rhythm which sets the tone, mood and tenor of the narrative. As in his earlier novel *The Circle of Reason*, Amitav Ghosh takes the narrative beyond the national frontiers and opens out the narrative to encompass experiences that are cosmopolitan. The quest for identity unfolds itself against the mood and background of a new internationalism. This new mood directs the protagonist's consciousness to new thresholds of experience.

These novel experiences are seen and understood through the narrator's consciousness. A distinct hue and message that eventually combine to make the quest meaningful mark each experience. The name of the narrator is not revealed, as a part of the narrative design, its aim is to suggest a contemporary consciousness, an all-encompassing identity. But at the same time the narrative subtly fuses personal experiences, to make the search a fascinating and living experience. As a young boy, his grandmother's passionate nationalism and her poignant nostalgic reminiscences of her life in East-Bengal, opens the narrator's mind to the meaning of nationalism and the unifying power of memory. As a young man he sees Ila's desperate attempts to accommodate herself to an alluring way of life in London, and her pathetic failure leads him to the realisation of the limitations and incomplete nature of such experiences. In short, neither of these two constitute a totality of experience. It is the enigmatic Tridib, who opens the narrator's consciousness to the power of imagination. This perception of the power of imagination helps him open his mind to new vistas of knowledge within and beyond the frontiers of this country. Armed with this superior imagination, the narrator sets out to forge an identity amidst the complex realities of a larger world.

At the outset, the grandmother holds sway over the narrator's sensibilities. Her strict disciplinarian exterior, which actually hides a tender heart, evokes in the young narrator awe and admiration. The story of her determined effort to forge a meaningful life after being widowed at a young age gives him an insight into the resilient quality of human beings. His grandmother seems to have risen from the depths of despair, literally from the proverbial ashes. Her tender reminiscences about her happy days of childhood and the heartbreak of the disintegration of their joint family are vividly transmitted through her imagination and memory. It captures the young narrator's imagination and makes it a living experience. This fact is well conveyed when he says:

> I could see Kana-babu's sweet shop at the end of their lane with absolute clarity, I could even see the pink cham-cham stacked in their trays. . . . I could hear the buzzing of the flies, and I could see Kana-babu sitting hunched behind his cash-box, scratching his stomach. (194)

The grandmother's stories of frustration and aspirations during the struggle for freedom expose the narrator's mind to the meaning of nationalism. He is astounded by her fierce determination and is over-awed by the nature of her involvement in the freedom struggle when she says, "I would have killed him [the English magistrate]. It was for our freedom: I would have done anything to be free." (39)

Tha'mma's illusions and the nostalgic feeling of comfort are soon shattered when she does visit Dhaka after a long time. As Sharmila Guha Majumdar aptly puts it: "Unlike so many of their brethren they did not have to feel the pang of being uprooted and to face the daunting task of rebuilding lives from the debris of history,"[28] consequently Tha'mma could cling to her nostalgic memories of her past. Her consciousness refuses to accept the new realities of life in the sub-continent. This illusion is soon shattered when she does visit Dhaka after a long time. Even before she starts for Dhaka she is confounded by the complex procedure she has to go through to visit her "Home." Quite unable to come to terms with aberrations like the partition, her questions about it have a childlike simplicity. She wants to know if she would be able to see the border between India and East Pakistan from the plane. She strongly believes that the physical division of the country would be indicated by "trenches perhaps, or soldiers, or guns pointing at each other, or even just barren strips of land." (151) She is even more confounded when her son tells her: "This is the modern world. The border isn't on the frontier; it's right inside the airport. You'll see. You will cross it when you have to fill in all those disembarkation cards and things." (151-52) As K. Damodar Rao says, "The myth of nationalism gets broken in the absence of these physical equivalents of the division."[29] She then wonders "What was all for then partition and all the killings and everything if there isn't something between?" (151)

It is an extremely poignant moment when she arrives in Dhaka her home and quickly realises that it is no more her home. Th'amma notices that everything has changed completely on the way to her sister Mayadebi's house, even as the driver points out to her the new theatres and hotels, just one refrain emerges from her lips, "It's all wonderful. But where is Dhaka?" (206) It clearly indicates the new profile of Dhaka which is alien to her. Like her, Jethomoshai stubbornly holds on to his conviction. He had chosen to ignore the shadow line, "Once you start moving you never stop. . . . I don't believe in this India-shindia . . . but I suppose when you get there they decide to draw another line somewhere? what will you do then?" (215) Her attempts to bring him back to Calcutta are gruesomely aborted on the streets of Dhaka during a mindless communal riot, a perpetual bane of the sub-continent. In the bargain she also loses her nephew Tridib who is dear to her. This mindless carnage has a devastating effect on her psyche. And as Novy Kapadia says, "Her home in Dhaka, which was like a pastoral retreat, a garden vision is now a reminder of death and communal border for the grandmother."[30] Commenting upon the episode of Tha'mma's visit to Dhaka, Girish Karnad says, "The grandmother's visit to the ancestral home along with Tridib and his English girl friend is surely one of the most memorable scenes in English fiction . . . past and future meet . . . leading to a shattering climax."[31] On returning to India, she is a completely changed woman, as the narrator's sharp perceptions quickly notice. She gives vent to her feeling of rancour when India goes to war with Pakistan. Novy Kapadia makes a pertinent observation in this context: "Her idyllic vision is shattered. The desire is changed. To use the phraseology of social Psychology, the grandmother also now thinks in terms of 'Us and them.'"[32] As a war donation she gives away her gold chain, her most valuable possession, as she now firmly believes that "We have to kill them before they kill us." (273)

Tha'mma also launches a scathing attack on Ila for her western ways and pretensions. She tells the narrator: "Ila has no right to live there [London] she doesn't belong there." (78)

This is one of the reasons for her being upset at the narrator's involvement with Ila, who she believes is hopelessly out of tune with her own life. The severity and associated heart aches of the struggle for freedom, India's war with China and Pakistan have all added up to severely restrict her sensibility and vision. Thus blinded by emotional nationalism, she holds out the alarming prospect that feelings of nationalism can only develop through the process of war and sustained bloodshed. The narrator perceives the limitations of her vision which is so sadly out of tune with the new cosmopolitan consciousness, because of its failure to take a larger world view.

The narrator's gradual realisation of the limitations of Tha'mma's vision is complemented by an equally clear understanding of the limitations of an entirely different vision represented by Ila.

As a child the narrator would await Ila's arrival from some fascinating distant country. To the boy, brought up within the humdrum routine of a small puritanical world Ila appears, in Nandita Sinha's words, "As an exotic butterfly with easy intimacy with places which are magic names in the boy's atlas."[33] Even as children they are miles apart in their understanding and perception of places. Ila, in spite of having travelled so extensively, had merely moved without seeing, and on the other hand the narrator in spite of not having travelled at all, had the ability of seeing places through his superior imagination, a gift bequeathed to him by his uncle Tridib. As a result, the narrator is able to convert those mundane places into exotic locales. Even as they grew up, Ila's perceptions had not changed whereas the narrator's perceptions and assimilation had become keener. This aspect is well illustrated years later, when the narrator goes to London to collect data from the India office library on the textile trade between India and England in the 19th century and mentions Cairo to Ila. All that she could remember was that "ladies" in the airport "was on the other side of the departure lounge." (20) The narrator had conjured on the other hand in his mind the enigmatic Pyramids and had wished to touch them. The reasons for Ila's failure to react are summed up by Tridib when he says, "The inventions she lived in moved with her, so that although she lived in many places, she had never travelled at all." (21)

As a child the narrator had also been fascinated by her life in London and intrigued by her stories about Nick Price, the son of their old family friends, the Prices. It is only later that he realises that her stories were concocted, especially about Nick Price. Even as a child she had hidden the essentially mean and the timid in Nick Price. She relates one harrowing incident of racial prejudice, where she projects Nick Price as a knight in shining armour rescuing a damsel in distress, herself. In reality he had run away from the scene for fear and embarrassment at being seen with a non-white. Even when she grows up, she persists with her self-delusion and does not hesitate to marry him, despite his proven qualities of inconsistency and waywardness. When the narrator goes to London and gets to observe her life from close quarters, he is saddened by the mess she has made of her life due to her own stubborn refusal to face reality. What she thought was liberation, from a middle class culture was nothing but a camouflage for a servile obsession with western culture. As Louis James says, "Ila desires freedom from a middle class orthodoxy, but she discovers that the free world she had tried to build for herself was not free from the squalor of betrayal."[34] Thus her love for a man like Nick Price and her marriage to him can only be construed as a desperate attempt to clutch on to a way of life she has glamourised, for which Nick Price is a gateway. Ila's inability to assimilate the rich pageantry of the world is one basic flaw in her consciousness, the other being her inability to assimilate the past or envisage the future. As a result, neither the Lelt Book House with a rich past nor Cairo with its majestic and awe inspiring Pyramids fail to evoke any vibrant response from her.

Ila's attempt to identify herself with the western world is highly incongruous. This idea is brought to the fore when in London the narrator identifies the building in which Alan Tresawsen and his friends Dan, Mike, and Franscesca had stayed during the World War, much to the astonishment of Ila and Nick. The mood during the World War then becomes the bone of contention between Ila and the narrator. Ila believes that Tresawsen and his friends shared a particular kind of happiness during the war in spite of the turbulent times. But the narrator strongly disputes it. This confrontation leads to a highly presumptuous lecture by Ila, where she believes that she and her companions in Southwell would be a part of the future just as Tresawsen and his friends had been. It is a blatant contradiction of her sensibility, as she does not value the future. She is dismissive of the insignificant life led by the narrator in a country where according to her nothing significant happened except for riots, floods and famines. Her misplaced conceptions expose her limitations about politics and its seriousness. Interestingly her friends do not take her too seriously. To them she is merely a decorative piece nothing more than "our own upper-class Asian Marxist" (97) in short a non-entity. Ila, it is clear, is living in a world of self-deception and shallowness. Another example of her shallowness is her taking up a job with children's organisation without any liking for children. She is ultimately out of tune with both the worlds, the native as well as the adopted, and sadly ends up belonging to neither. Ila's seeming cosmopolitanism only ends in her losing her own identity in an attempt to ape a borrowed one.

In a subtle juxtaposition, the author projects May Price as her alter ego. Her cosmopolitanism is real. In spite of being firmly ensconced in the western sensibility she, unlike Ila, is able to respond to other realities. Her trip to India on Tridib's invitation initiates her into realities of a different kind in the sub-continent. May is quick to respond to the new ethos as can be seen in the incident at the railway station when she meets Tridib for the first time. It is very clear from the outset that she is a broad-minded uncomplicated person. May's belief in certain life convictions is best illustrated through her action in relieving a street dog of its misery with the help of Tridib and the narrator on the streets of Calcutta. Her convictions suffer a severe jolt when she attempts to rescue on the streets of Dhaka, Jethamoshai and Khalil, the rickshaw man from a bloodthirsty mob. She is horrified at the new aspect of reality in the sub-continent. May blames herself for the gruesome death of Tridib, Khalil, and Jethamoshai. And for the rest of her life she makes a sincere attempt to understand this reality.

On the personal level, the narrator shares an excellent rapport with her. Even as a child he had been fascinated by her. As he grew older, he could not fathom the depth of the relation between her and Tridib. He comes to view her as a simple and uncomplicated person. Many years later in London he meets her and is impressed by her sincere approach towards life. Unlike Ila and her friends, she is truly committed, and without pretensions, to social service. May spends long hours standing in street corners, raising money for the needy. Possessed of an interest in Third World causes, she goes beyond Oxfam. The narrator, who is himself a participant in one such drive, observes her total involvement in the cause, going about the work without a feeling of superiority, or a patronising attitude. May's weekly fast in order to experience the pangs of hunger from which a part of the world suffers has a ring of sincerity about it, and is in total contrast to Ila's artificiality. May Price is the redeeming consciousness in a world surrounded by misconceptions and distorted visions. Despite his misbehaviour with her, she is still warm towards the narrator, and redeems him by her affection which is an integral part of her nature. Ila had dismissed his sincere love with a patronising "you were the brother I never had." (111) His dejected love finds solace in May's sincere affection.

In the end, it is May who reveals to him the truth about Tridib's death. She pours her heart out to him, holding herself responsible for Tridib's death. May corrects this misconception when she fully understands the nature of Tridib's sacrifice. May's sincere endeavour to come to terms with new realities coupled with the simple design of her life makes a lasting impression on the narrator's mind. Ila and May, the narrator realises, are alter egos, in the sense that they represent a pseudo cosmopolitanism and a truly cosmopolitan consciousness respectively.

The assimilation of Tridib's cosmopolitan vision into the consciousness of the narrator forms the concluding portion of the search for identity.

Tridib, the narrator's uncle, is easily the most unusual character in the novel. His enigmatic presence not only pervades the whole novel but also lends credence to the human drama and narrative design. To the narrator, even as a child, Tridib is his undisputed hero, in spite of his grandmother terming him a "loafer and wastrel." Tridib's encyclopaedic knowledge combined with a streak of intensely worldly shrewdness has the ability to transform mundane and monotonous street corners into places of interest and fascination. Tridib introduces him to the fascinating world of the imagination. He expands the frontiers of his boyhood world giving him worlds to travel and eyes to see with. Tridib had always advised him to use his imagination with precision. And as Nandita Sinha says, "The narrator learns to value the imagination as revealing a world as concrete and real and infinitely more exciting than the world experienced through the senses."[35] This aspect comes to the fore when his keen imaginative perceptions are pitted against Ila's lack of imagination. As a result Colombo acquires a new dimension and equally memorable is the narrator's vision of war torn London. Many years later, in London, the recollection is vivid. Although he could not see the uprooted trees or splintered windows or buckled flagstones that have been lost in a forty year old past, he realises that he has been shown something more valuable—England in her finest hour. As the narrator says: "Despite the clear testimony of my eyes it seemed to me still that Tridib had shown something truer about Solent road a long time ago in Calcutta." (57) Thus, in spite of it being his first trip to London, he identifies each and every place with precision and passion, much to the astonishment of Ila and Nick Price. The whole panorama comes with a photographic clarity on the screen of his imagination. Thus Tridib's advice of:

> knowing through desire, real desire, which was not the same thing as greed or lust, a pure, painful and primitive desire, a longing for everything that was not in oneself, a torment of the flesh, that carried one beyond the limits of one's mind to other times and other places and even, if one was lucky, to a place where there was no border between oneself and one's image in the mirror. (29)

is fully realised and assimilated in the narrator's consciousness. It emphasises the point that Tridib is the chief architect in shaping the narrator's consciousness. To the others, including his own family members who failed to gauge his depth, May Price with her cosmopolitan vision comes into his life like a breath of fresh air. Her involvement with Tridib is deep in spite of it being an unusual relationship. In Tridib's company May is exposed to new realities in the subcontinent. Her sensitive and humane attitude towards life is evident, when she puts a street dog out of its misery on the streets of Calcutta unmindful of the danger to her own life. Tridib's question, if she would do the same thing for him if he ever needed it, serves as a premonition of his own death.

As Tridib makes the trip to Dhaka along with Tha'mma and May Price to bring back Jethamoshai, a more sinister drama unfolds itself in the sub-continent which ultimately brings to the fore the gruesome realities of partition. May Price is witness to Tridib's death at the hands of a bloodthirsty mob, on the streets of Dhaka. She holds herself responsible for his death and carries that guilt in her conscience. In London fifteen years later, the narrator is told the truth about his death by Robi and May Price.

The narrator is shocked beyond words. Robi's sense of disgust and despair comes out when he says, "Why don't they draw thousands of little lines through the whole sub-continent and give every little place a new name?" (241) The last story told by Tridib to him before leaving for Dhaka about a hero called Tristem, a man without a country, who fell in love with a woman across the sea, signifying a world without borders, becomes achingly relevant to the present time which endlessly harps on boundaries.

May Price and the narrator realise that Tridib had sacrificed his life, had deliberately plunged into the mob knowing fully well that death would be imminent. Her guilt is dispelled when she realises the true heroism of his sacrifice; in which her contribution had been insignificant. Tridib's death is a parable of our times. It shows the increasing violence besieging the sub-continent, violence engendered by demarcations of class, caste and creed.

The narrator in his search for identity realises that Tha'mma and Ila represent a narrowness of vision and pseudo-cosmopolitanism respectively. It is May's humanism combined with Tridib's vision, that can mould the psyche of the contemporary consciousness. It can be noticed that Tha'mma's ties are based on physical, highly emotional bonds whereas Tridib's vision is based more on the imaginative and the intellect. It is only when the window of the mind opens out to a larger world, but with the roots firmly embedded, does the search for identity become fruitful and meaningful.

These various experiences help the narrator to realise that identity is not limited to natural geographic boundaries but goes beyond its realms, to root itself in a wider world. The author presents this realisation not through direct commentary or explanation but through an unobtrusive juxtaposition of a variety of world views.

V

Upamanyu Chatterjee's maiden novel, *English, August: An*

Indian Story has been described by C. Sengupta as "a subtle metaphor of contemporary youth's quest for self realisation."[36]

The novel has a brilliant visual appeal by virtue of its photographic descriptions of places and situations. Long after the novel is over, the mind continues to visualise the setting and the story in all its minute details.

The novel can be read at two levels. On the surface level, the book is a commentary on the administrative services of India, the corruption in high places, the high-handedness, inefficiency, the oppressiveness of the system, its utter indifference to the eradication of social evils, the acute class consciousness among the IAS hierarchy, the little snobberies and petty jealousies. At the deeper level, it is an exposition of the predicament of the modern youth in this vast and complex country. There is a sense of dislocation and a general meaninglessness, as a result the protagonist's search for identity is sometimes pathetic, sometimes humorous, even ridiculous. However it ultimately turns out to be a journey from rootlessness to maturity, in short, a struggle to come to terms with oneself against the complex realities of this country.

The crux of Agastaya's quest lies in striking a balance between his megalopolitan sensibilities and the realities of life in a backward town of this country. Madna, a provincial town, serves as the background to Agastaya's quest. The protagonist of the novel, Agastaya Sen, is a megalopolitan youth, educated in the best public schools of Darjeeling, whose schedule and life style turns topsy-turvy when he reports in Madna as an IAS trainee officer. Right from the first day in Madna, Agastaya suffers from a sense of rootlessness. The reason for this rootlessness is not too hard to perceive. As Meenakshi Raykar comments, "His background has been a very powerful alienating force which has left a sense of displacement."[37] His elitist education and the frivolous luxuries afforded by cities like Calcutta and Delhi have obviously conditioned his mind to just one way of life. Nissim Ezekiel has perceptively pointed out, "It is Agastaya's Darjeeling School that establishes his alienation of which he remains conscious virtually through this Indian story."[38] For people like

Agastaya who have no special devouring interests and very little ambition, the megalopolitan cities are the right places to live in, for they afford them the luxury of anonymity. In Madna he can no more remain anonymous and by virtue of being an IAS officer, he is a demi god, and thus the focus of attention. This change demands a re-orientation of his perception of himself and of his life. Agastaya finds himself in the type of places he had read about only in newspapers—"places where floods and caste wars occurred, entire harijan families were murdered." (4) This disparity between the two worlds obviously creates a strong sense of dislocation in the protagonist. The novelist himself spells out his protagonist's predicament:

> Anchorlessness that was to be his chaotic concern in that uncertain year, battling a sense of waste was to be another fodder too, in the forrago of his mind, self pity in an uncongenial clime, the incertitude of his reactions to Madna, his job, and his ability to relate to it—other abstractions too, his niche in the world, his future—the elusive mocking nature of happiness, the possibility of its attainment. (24-25)

For a year Agastaya was to move from one room in the rest house to another room in some other house; it was homelessness of a kind, a physical manifestation of an inner sense of restlessness. His experiences on the first day consisting of an integration meeting, the sea of humanity waiting for justice around the collector's office, the collector's overbearing manner leaving him with a lambent dullness. As a result Agastaya's new life begins on a note of despondency. He is out of tune with his surroundings, as he had feared at the outset, when he felt "I'd much rather act in a porn film than be a bureaucrat. But I suppose one has to live." (3) His accommodation in the rest house is drab and uninteresting and to add to his woes, is an indifferent cook Vasant who serves him insipid meals. A painting by an amateur artist Tamse, an ex-engineer, hanging in his room gives him his first lesson about loneliness. Tamse's painting, mediocre as a work of art, was a sincere attempt to recreate home, and his poem behind it brought out his loneliness. It was the attempt on Tamse's part to share a mood, an experience, which turns Agastaya's initial reaction of indignation at the painting, to one of sympathy and understanding. Agastaya had always wanted to be alone but had not bargained for this kind of loneliness. The initial response to the discord between his past and present is that of escapism. Agastaya feels the urge to get away from the stifling bureaucratic ambience to the comfort of a secret life in the rest house. Drab and dull though it is, to him it is more actual and exciting than the world outside. Thus Agastaya begins to lead three lives in Madna, "The official with its social concomitance, the unofficial, which included boozing with Shankar and Sathe and later with Bhatia, and the secret in the universe of his room, which encompasses jogging by moonlight." (48) The attempt to juggle with three lives enhances his sense of dislocation. However, his sense of smugness and unconscious pride in the thought that he alone felt dislocated is soon dispelled. His inter-action with Bhatia reveals to him that he is not the only one afflicted with this syndrome. In the months of adjustment, he writes several times to his father about his feeling of dislocation. All the time there is no real involvement either in his social or official life, as he feels that his situation is somehow unreal, and just a temporary sojourn in Madna. He goes through the motions of a hectic social life without it making any impression. The sense of bewilderment is even stronger in his official inter-actions. Appreciating the commitment of men like Srivastav, while deploring what Vinay Lal refers to as "lording it over the millions"[39] he is confused about his place in the bureaucratic set-up. In Madna, he is exposed to the petty power play of the bureaucracy which allows a woman like Mrs. Srivastav to impose her half-baked knowledge on hapless victims. The inability to reconcile this reality with his father's inspiring vision of an IAS officer's responsibility aggravates his feeling of anchorlessness. As a result he found it difficult to read and assimilate anything when the mind was in such turmoil. Among all the books that Agastaya carried with him, Marcus Aurelius afforded him some measure of comfort. He identified with the wise sad Roman as both of them were concerned "not with the soul squashing problems of being poor but the exhilarating abstract problems of one immersed wholly in his self." (68) The fact that Agastaya seeks solace in an ancient Roman writer exposes his pseudo-intellectualism and the urge to escape from concrete realities of life in Madna.

In spite of his determined effort to avoid involvement, certain encounters hold out the possibilities of other solutions. Shankar, an executive engineer who also feels banished in Madna, abandons his destiny to goddess Jagadamba. Agastaya is however unable to identify with this determinist philosophy. Equally unacceptable is the attitude of the judge, which is as fatalist as Shankar's philosophy. Having already spent a considerable period of time in Madna, the judge is yet unable to grapple with the feeling of dislocation. He feels that, for him, salvation is only possible with his retirement. To Agastaya, this holds out an alarming possibility for his own future. The notion embodied in the judge, that "age was in no way connected with the intensity of a sense of dislocation" (89) carries the temptation "to slink away from having to think, to wish to be that pair of ragged claws that had so tantalised him in his college years, scuttling over the floors of the silent seas" (114) carries a warning for Agastaya—the necessity of finding a constructive solution to his own sense of dislocation. A small but decisive turn occurs when he meets Govinda Sathe, a cartoonist by profession, hence called the "Joker of Madna." Sathe gives Agastaya a copy of the *Bhagvad Gita* and insists that he read it. Agastaya had always associated the *Gita* with age, when the after life begins to look important. As a result he approached the *Gita* with a degree of apprehension. Agastaya read those passages in the *Gita* which discussed the problem of the restless mind, where Krishna tells Arjuna: "It is indeed hard to train. But by constant practice and by freedom from passions, the mind in truth can be trained." (83) He had earlier taken recourse to Marcus Aurelius, finding in problems a bonding with the ancient Roman philosopher. On the other hand, the *Gita* offers the possibilities of solutions. Although unable to comprehend many obtruse passages, he implicitly understands that it can unfold solutions to his problems. This shows Agastaya's newly formed desire to look for solutions rather than brood on the problems. It is thus a positive step in Agastaya's quest for identity.

Another positive development is Agastaya's acknowledgement that he has become more perceptive and sensitive in Madna. His first trip into the district opens his eyes to new realities. In retrospect he realises that in Delhi and in Calcutta, he was insensitive to his surroundings as he was "busy with trivia, talking rubbish with someone, filled with impatience to get somewhere in time for something . . . his mind was just too cluttered up for him to notice anything." (123) In spite of these positive indications, his frustrations continued to build up, slowly rising to a crescendo. The rains came to Madna, refreshed and put new life in everything around it. But Agastaya's mind continued to be restless and unsettled. His bureaucratic life—the over-bearing presence of Srivastav and Kumar with their intimidating behaviour, his social life with its trivialities are both equally unsatisfying. In such a mood, "he was enraged at himself for not having planned his life with intelligence, for having dared to believe that he was adaptable enough to any job and circumstances for not knowing how to change either, for wasting time." (112) He felt that he was neither master of his fate nor time. Agastaya strongly felt that most men like him "chose in ignorance and fretted in an uncongenial world, they ultimately ended up compromising with or without grace or slipped into despair." (113-14) His anger is also directed at the failure of reason to direct significant action. He who had earlier believed in the power of reason begins to question its efficacy. He frets: "I want to know in the present, he said to himself, I want my reason, and not even my intuition, but my reason to tell me, here, you are now master of your time to come, act accordingly." (113) Agastaya resolves that reason is incapable of answering overwhelming questions. At the same time he also realises much to his dismay that all human relationships are futile; he comes to believe that all human beings are cocoons, all engrossed in themselves and that no one is anyone's confidant. The realisation dawns on him that he is alone in his quest for identity. The contrast between his life in Madna and in Calcutta and Delhi exposes the shallowness of his existence. The feeling of loneliness starts haunting him. He writes to his father saying that he could not get used to the job and that he was wasting his time. He also indicates in his letter that he would also like to change his job. Under the cumulative effect of overwhelming questions for which he finds no answers, his mind reaches a state of stasis. In that state of stasis, he stops analysing himself. The mind was restless due to the constant flux of warring thoughts which wracked his indeterminate mind. Earlier he had worried about the future but now he could not see it at all, engulfed as it was in a void. Life had suddenly become a black and serious business "with a tantalising painfully elusive, definite but checked goal, how to crush the restlessness of the mind." (135) Unable to confront this reality, his static mind had even contemplated suicide as a release from this burden that too he felt required too much effort. Very strangely he did not long for a megalopolitan life. He missed nothing, felt no contempt for the world; all that he wanted was "peace." The idea that men were sometimes masters of their fate now teased and haunted him. He felt that the precious seconds of his life were ticking away uselessly and that his unhappiness proportionately increasing every moment, with the bitter agony of not being able to confront it. Agastaya wondered if he should resign himself to fate or else take solace in the words of an ancient Hindu poem which held that "action is better than inaction." To get away from everything was Agastaya's immediate concern. In that state of mind, action is interpreted as escape from Madna. The trip to Delhi is thus regarded as an opportunity to recast his life's design, little realising that he is once again relapsing into escapism. Agastaya departs to Delhi with the thought that he did not want challenges or responsibility, but just to be happy, to lie on the roof of his house in Delhi and be immersed in himself.

Agastaya's sojourn in Delhi marks another significant step in his quest for identity. The trip elicits unexpected perspectives which shake his newfound faith that escape from Madna would solve his problems of restlessness. In Delhi, Agastaya, to his dismay, discovers that his bosom friend Dhrubo, is unhappy with the unreal nature of his job in the corporate world and is even contemplating joining the IAS. His indignation when told of Agastaya's desire to quit his job is evident when he remarks: "Just who and where do you think you are, an American taking an year off after college to discover himself?" (153) His cousin Tonic's anger is equally clear when he admonishes Agastaya, telling him that leaving such a job "is a ridiculously high price to pay for trying to regain some of the shallow pleasures of your past life." (170) He suggests that as an IAS officer, he has a real chance to do something constructive about the social system. Madan, his other college friend, is also deeply frustrated with his job in a chartered accountant's office. These encounters rather than reassuring him as expected places his mind in further turmoil. He realises that restlessness crosses the boundaries of place, that his friends in Delhi were as restless as he had been in Madna. The illusion that Madna was the source of his restlessness is soon dispelled. The sight of people sticking out like tongues from over-crowded buses, brings home to him the contrast between the concrete realities of their predicament and the nebulous nature of his own condition. The expectations of reassurance, with which he had come to Delhi remaining unfulfilled, he returns to Madna with his mind in even greater turmoil.

Back in Madna, his mind is, for the first time, open to positive influences. He is stirred by the single-minded dedication of John Avery, the English man who had travelled over half the globe to pursue a dream-to pay respects at his grandfather's grave in a remote place. He is moved by Baba Ramanna's labour of love, his rehabilitation of lepers, "a singular story of the immensity of human ambition" (235) and the Naxalites' fiery determination to create social awareness and to put an end to the exploitation of the tribals. He is influenced by Dr. Darshan Multani's sense of satisfaction and happiness in his chosen profession. His identification with the myth of the fisher king, where the fisher king is able to resolve his problems and divine a meaning in life, is another positive step in this stage of his quest for identity.

The opportunity to give a concrete shape to these positive inclinations comes with his posting to Jompanna as the Block Development officer. The bureaucratic hauteur and the inefficacy of the entire set up which had so deeply troubled him in Madna is neutralised in the obscure tribal village of Chipanthi. The sincerity of his efforts and his human understanding rise above the artificial barriers of language. Chipanthi brings him face to face with the soul-rending realities of life where "tribal parents were compelled to risk the lives of their children for half buckets of mud." (259) which passed off for water. Agastaya's first constructive step is taken when, over-riding official apathy and insensitivity, he finds a solution to their acute water problem. He is warmly appreciated for his timely action; the farewell accorded to him by the people of Jompanna is replete with affection. Back in Madna, Sathe's words of wisdom "whatever you choose to do, you will regret everything or regret nothing. Remember you're not James Bond, you only live once," (285) strikes the decisive chord in Agastaya's mind. The lure of a lotus eating life, escaping responsibility and action, is banished from his mind. He realises that the crux of his search for identity and the solution for his restlessness lies in coming to terms with the harsh realities of life in the sub-continent. The feeling that life is lying on the terrace to seeing the lives of children being risked for what appears to be a bucket of water has been one long odyssey for Agastaya. As David Kerr comments, "Sen undergoes a slow awakening from a life of self-centered sensuality into an awareness of human suffering and human responsibility."[40] Nevertheless, the hope that this new awareness will at some time help him to succeed in his quest for identity is a reassuring thought.

As Milan Kundera comments in the course of an interview, "It is through action that man steps forth from the repetitive universe. . . . It is through action that he distinguishes himself from others and becomes an individual."[41] This comment can be applied to what happens to Agastaya. The fulfillment of the quest for identity for him is definitely not too far away.

The study of the theme of the search for identity attempted in this chapter thus constantly reinforces the transnational and cosmopolitan scope of the novel of the Eighties. The protagonists are invariably presented as cultural travellers moving freely in a frontierless world. They have to forge their identities against the background of this new consciousness, coming to terms with the sheer expanse—geographical, cultural, intellectual and psychological—which constitute the complex contemporary reality. The effect of this concern is seen in an exhilarating openness which clearly demarcates the novel of the Eighties from its predecessors. The themes of the East-West encounter or the spiritual quest which were in the forefront in the earlier depictions now appear obsolete.

Another significant difference in the search is the refusal of the new novelists to consider retreat as a viable solution to the protagonist's dilemma. Almost all the major earlier novels dealing with this theme—R.K. Narayan's *The Guide*, Raja Rao's *The Serpent and the Rope*, Arun Joshi's *The Stranger Case of Billy Biswas*—take recourse to withdrawal from the world around them. Such a solution appears simplistic, almost escapist, in contrast to the new protagonist's determination to grapple with the reality, however confusing or problematic. The world in which the protagonists have to realise their identities is dynamic, constantly in motion, unlike the comparatively static world of the past. The solution in the new novels is in terms of looking ahead or moving forward rather than withdrawal or retreat. While protagonists in the earlier novels increasingly disassociated themselves from the world around them, their counterparts in the new novel conversely move towards an increasing association and communication. From the midnight children's conference to Picture Singh, Saleem's life has been one long endeavour to forge links with his fellow human beings. Although Omar Khayyam Shakil in *Shame* begins with a self-centred approach to living, his search for identity turns positive with his association with Sufiya Zenobia. Alu's Quest in *The Circle of Reason* is series of associations starting in Lalpukur in Bengal moving through al-Ghazira and culminating in El Oued. The unnamed narrator similarly finds himself in a chain of associations which take him from Calcutta to London. Agastaya Sen in *English, August,* too realises that disassociation from his surroundings cannot provide peace of mind. Meaning in life can only be found through positive action and interaction with others as he realises through his experiences in a remote tribal village.

A realisation of this importance of association, communication and positive action leads to the most significant factor of the search for identity in the novel of the Eighties, its emphasis on the basic element, human compassion and fellow feeling. The technical virtuosity of these novels often results in an over-emphasis on the stylistic pyrotechnics. A sensitive reading of the texts however elicits the contrast between the glossiness of technique and the simplicity of the ultimate message. In spite of the search for identity taking the protagonists through various continents, countries and cultures, the solution is startlingly simple. Paradoxically, it is practical and realistic, drawing attention to a basic element of human existence. The search for identity in the protagonists is ultimately linked with a discovery of compassion within themselves and others. The crux of a truly cosmopolitan culture revolves on this pivot of fellow feeling, binding disparate worlds together.

This perception can help us to view the novel of the Eighties from a hitherto unexplored angle. A mere geographical or intellectual expansion of the world cannot create an authentic cosmopolitan consciousness, we need to erase the 'Shadow Lines' in our minds.

NOTES

1. R.S. Pathak, "Identity Crisis in the Novels of Salman Rushdie," *Quest for Identity in Indian English Writing*, Part 1: Fiction, ed. R.S. Pathak (New Delhi: Bahri, 1992), p. 112.
2. Deval Dharkar, "Discussion on *Midnight's Children*," *New Quest*, 36 (1982), p. 350.

3. M.K. Naik, "The Life of Fragments: The Fate of Identity in *Midnight's Children*," *Studies in Indian English Literature* (New Delhi: Sterling, 1987), p. 46.
4. Dieter Reimenschneider, "History and the Individual in Anita Desai's *Clear light of Day* and Salman Rushdie's *Midnight's Children*," *The New Indian Novel in English*, ed. Viney Kirpal (New Delhi: Allied, 1990), p. 194.
5. Salman Rushdie, Interview by Anna Rutherford, *Kunapipi*, 4.2 (1982), p. 24.
6. R.S. Pathak, "Salman Rushdie's Treatment of Alienation," *Indian Fiction in English: Problems and Promises*, ed. R.S. Pathak (New Delhi: Northern Book Center, 1990), p. 167.
7. Michael Murphy, *Grefin the Kingdom* (New York: Dell, 1972), p. 11.
8. Mario Couto, "The Search for Identity," *The Eye of the Beholder: Indian Writing in English*, ed. Maggie Butcher (London: Commonwealth Institute, 1983), p. 63.
9. Salman Rushdie, *Imaginary Homelands* (New York: Viking Penguin, 1991), p. 16.
10. Ron Blabber, *CRNLE Review*, 2 (1982), p. 63.
11. Timothy Hyman, "Fairy Tale Agitprop," *London Magazine* (October 1983), p. 40.
12. M.D. Fletcher, "Rushdie's *Shame* as Apologue," *The Journal of Commonwealth Literature*, 21.1, 1986, p. 123.
13. Salman Rushdie, PW Interviews, *Publishers Weekly*, Nov. 11, 1983.
14. Griffith A. Chausee, "A Textual Unicorn: Identity and Islamic Reference in Salman Rushdie's *Shame*," *The Toronto South Asian Review*, 8.3 (1990), p. 25.
15. Michael Hollington, "Salman Rushdie's *Shame*," *Meanjin Quarterly*, 3 Sept. 1984, p. 405.
16. Fawzia Afzal Khan, "Post-Modernist Strategies of Liberation in the works of Salman Rushdie," *Journal of South Asian Literature*, 23.1 (1988), p. 141.
17. Sushila Singh, "*Shame*: Salman Rushdie's Judgement on Pakistan," *Studies in Indian Fiction in English*, ed. G.S. Balarama Gupta (Gulbarga: JIWE, 1987), p. 17.
18. Hollington, p.406.
19. D.B. Jewison, rev. of *Shame*, *The Toronto South Asian Review*,

2.3 (1984), p. 79.
20. M.D. Fletcher, *Journal of Indian Writing in English*, 21.1 (1986), p. 124.
21. Paul Sharrad, "The Outburst of the Imagination," *CRNLE Review*, 2 (1984), p. 25.
22. S. Sengupta, "An Allegorical *Tom Jones*: An Analysis of Amitav Ghosh's *The Circle of Reason*," *Recent Indian Fiction*, ed. R.S. Pathak (New Delhi: Prestige, 1994), p. 28.
23. James Clifford, "The Transit Lounge of Culture," *Times Literary Supplement*, 4956, 3 May 1991, pp. 7-8.
24. Robert Dixon, "Travelling in the West: The Writing of Amitav Ghosh," *The Journal of Commonwealth Literature*, 31.1 (1996), p. 8.
25. Fakhrul Alam, "Amitav Ghosh (1956—)," *Writers of the Indian Diaspora: A Bio-bibliographical Source*, ed. Nelson Emmanuel (Connecticut: Greenwood Press, 1993), p. 138.
26. Dixon, p. 6.
27. G.J.V. Prasad, "The Unfolding of a Raga: Narrative Structure in *The Circle of Reason*," *The New Indian Novel in English*, ed. Kirpal, p. 103.
28. Sharmila Guha Majumdar, "Amitav Ghosh's *The Shadow Lines* and *In an Antique Land*: Some Thematic Considerations," *Indian Literature Today*, Vol. 1: Drama and Fiction, ed. R.K. Dhawan (New Delhi: Prestige, 1994), p. 146.
29. K. Damodar Rao, "Silence as Possible Mode of Response in Amitav Ghosh's *The Shadow Lines*," *Kakatiya Journal of English Studies*, Vol. 13 (1993), p. 83.
30. Novy Kapadia, "Imagination and Politics in Amitav Ghosh's *Shadow Lines*," *The New Indian Novel in English*, ed. Kirpal, p. 203.
31. Girish Karnad, "Worlds within Worlds," Rev. of *The Shadow Lines*, *Indian Express Magazine*, 18 Dec. 1988, p. 5.
32. Kapadia, p. 203.
33. Nandita Sinha, "Perspectives in Times: The Narrator as Child in Amitav Ghosh's *The Shadow Lines*," *Indian Literature Today*, ed. Dhawan, p. 180.
34. Louis James, "Shadow Lines: Cross-Cultural Perspectives in the Fiction of Amitav Ghosh," *Indian Literature Today*, ed. Dhawan, p. 155.

35. Sinha, p. 181.
36. C. Sengupta, "Upamanyu Chatterjee's *English, August*: Metaphor of Contemporary Youth's Quest for Self-Realisation," *Indian Literature Today*, Vol. 1, ed. Dhawan, p. 110.
37. Meenakshi Raykar, "The Intellectual in a State of 'Anomy': *No Longer at Ease* and *English, August: An Indian Story*," *New Quest*, 92 (1992), p. 110.
38. Nissim Ezekiel, *Indian Post*, 21 Aug 1988.
39. Vinay Lal, "Enjoyable Reading," rev. of *English, August: An Indian Story* by Upamanyu Chatterjee, *Indian Literature*, 33.3 (1990), p. 156.
40. David Kerr, "History and the Possibilities of Choice: A Study of Anita Desai's *Baumgartner's Bombay*, Upamanyu Chatterjee's *English, August* and Shashi Deshpande's *That Long Silence*," *Indian Women Novelists*, Vol. 1, ed. R.K. Dhawan (New Delhi: Prestige), p. 129.
41. Milan Kundera, *The Art of the Novel*, trans. Linda Aster (New Delhi: Rupa, 1995), p. 23.

Techniques in Modern Indian Fiction

A historical survey of the Indian English novel shows that the configuration of the novel has changed from time to time, reflecting the changes in the age, context and the perception of the writer. The Indian English novel can be marked into three distinct phases. The first phase comprises novels imitating the romantic novels of Scott. The 1930s mark the second phase, with the novel coming into its own and establishing an independent identity. The third phase unmistakably begins with the 1980s, with the novel blazing a new trail.

It is logical to conjecture that the early novels with their staid themes had hardly any scope for experimentation with technique. A shift in the mood was witnessed in the 1930s, when the nationalist movement was gradually gaining momentum and was reaching a feverish pitch. The three important novelists of the time, Mulk Raj Anand, Raja Rao, and R.K. Narayan wrote with a compelling sense of urgency, giving expression to the fiery voice of a colonized nation. Hence they can be considered as the real inaugurators of the form. William Walsh's comments on the three writers in their depiction of themes, characters and use of English as mentioned in the earlier chapter give a comprehensive picture of the new beginnings in the novel genre.

However even at that time, experiments with technique were limited. As Novy Kapadia comments, "Prior to Rushdie, technical innovations by Indian novelists in English, were limited, restricted and in the embryonic form."[1] The first experiment with technique can be seen in Raja Rao. He is, according to Uma Parameswaran, "the guru of an experimental style."[2] In his novel *Kanthapura*, Raja Rao uses a garrulous grandmother as the narrator. A direct adaptation from the vernacular to English, a technical experiment hitherto untried, gives the narrative a racy rhythm. This synchronization of two diverse languages anticipates similar experimentation in the later novels. R.K. Narayan is another writer who experiments cautiously with narrative technique in his novel *The Guide* (1958). The constant forward and backward movement replaces the straightforward narrative. He also experiments with the flashback and montage technique used often in cinematography.

Chaman Nahal's *Azadi* experiments for the first time with the technique of the multiple narrator. A novel on the Partition, this technique is used to give the reader a more sweeping and greater grasp of reality, successfully highlighting the inner tension between diverse points of view and raising numerous socio-moral, ethical and eternal human questions, through the multiple-narrator technique It is this multiple-narrator technique that sets apart *Azadi* from the other novels on the theme of Partition written so far.

For the development of the Indian English novel, the contribution of G.V. Desani is significant. The novel *All about H. Hatterr* is full of Indian-Englishisms seen in hybrid lexical collocations and syntactic variations. Rushdie himself admits to the tremendous influence of Desani on his writing. According to Uma Parameswaran, "It is G.V. Desani who is Rushdie's avowed master as he showed how English could be bent and kneaded until it spoke in an authentically Indian voice."[3]

Experimentation in technique, hitherto sporadic in the Indian English novel, suddenly explodes with full force with *Midnight's Children*. The trend is sustained, although in a less flamboyant manner, in the works of other novelists of the Eighties like Amitav Ghosh's and Upamanyu Chatterjee's. Combining the new with the old, Rushdie's technique heralds the coming of a new genre giving it a truly cosmopolitan identity. This uninhibited experimentation with narrative technique and the flexible use of English language provided the genre of the Indian English novel a new direction and renewed confidence. William Walsh succinctly analyses Rushdie's intriguingly complex narrative technique:

> Combining the elements of magic and fantasy, the grimmest realism, extravagant farce, multimirrored analogy and a potent symbolic structure, Salman Rushdie has captured the astonishing energy of the novel unprecedented in scope, manner and achievement in the hundred and fifty year old tradition of the Indian novel in English.[4]

The novel of the 1980s brings to the fore a new cosmopolitanism in its exploration of the complex nature of human experience. It deals with transnational, transcontinental and transcultural experiences. It projects the human struggle to come to terms with a new cosmopolitan reality. These variegated experiences are too complex and multi-dimensional to be given expression through a linear narrative. As the experiences became more and more complex, the novelists too found it imperative to give expression to their perceptions through new techniques. Irving H. Buchen also makes a similar observation: "The essential pressure for experimentation comes from the novelist's conviction that the demands of his vision are so new and urgent and the forms available so tired that new forms or hybrid must be created . . . all experiment entails the violation of known orders of sequence, Syntax, punctuation and language. The novelist plumbs for new forms only when he is driven up against a wall and nothing else works."[5] The new cosmopolitanism inevitably brings the novelists into contact with post-modernism. Hence the new novel is a hybrid, interfacing the age-old Indian techniques from the oral tradition to the latest in postmodernism. And like other postmodernist writers, the Indian English novelists too violate and confound traditional features. An element of playfulness, not found in the earlier novel is an important feature of the new writing. Myth, fantasy, the supernatural, snatches of songs, and movie scenes are the elements used in the new writing to give expression to the chaotic and complex nature of contemporary experience. The post-modernist novel redrafts the contract between the writer and reader. The authorial intrusions into the narrative are frequent, often violating the time sequence. Alterations in language sequence are numerous, resulting in a variety of possibilities in language usage. The compelling use of myth and fantasy in order to depict experiences that cannot be given expression in realistic terms is another important feature. All these post-modernist traits are significantly present in the new novel of the Eighties. The novelists of the Eighties combine traditional Indian narrative devices like episodicity, plotlessness and story-within-story with new post-modernist techniques. The characteristics of both traditions are relevant to the understanding of the quality and tone of Indian English fiction.

The oral narrative tradition has been an integral part of Indian literature through the ages. In a country with a strong folk culture and intrinsic religious inclinations, the oral narrative form has inevitably been a dominant mode of expression since times immemorial. Salman Rushdie, in an interview, acknowledges the tremendous influence of the Indian oral narrative tradition on his writing. In the course of an interview, he says:

> Listening to this man [a famous storyteller in Baroda] reminded me of the shape of the oral narrative. It's not linear. An oral narrative does not go from the beginning to the middle to the end of the story. It goes in great swoops; it goes in spirals or in loops. It every so often reiterates something that happened earlier to remind you and then takes you off again. Sometimes summarises itself, it frequently digresses off into something that the storyteller appears just to have thought of, then it comes back to the main thrust of the narrative . . . so that's what *Midnight's Children* was, I think every thing about Laurence Sterne, Garcia Marquez and all that comes a long way behind that I felt when writing it.[6]

This sums up the intricate structure on which Rushdie mounts *Midnight's Children*. Combining the oral tradition with post-modernist techniques, Rushdie compels us to take a new perception of the socio-political ethos of the sub-continent.

The narrative technique employed by Saleem, the protagonist of *Midnight's Children* is interestingly the same as employed by the traditional clown narrator (the Vidushka) in the ancient performance art of Kuttiyattam. To quote A. Paniker: "The Vidushka can take all kinds of liberties; in fact he is expected to and encouraged to do so. He can get lost in his own elaborations. He can turn his narrative into a string of short stories or take one of these stories and lengthen it for hours or days. Thus the oral narrative can easily achieve the length of a novel if length is a criterion at all . . . indulge in any kind of extravagance provided he can come back to the main thread of the narrative."[7]

Midnight's Children is seventy years of Indian history told by a loquacious Saleem to Padma an illiterate worker in the Braganza pickle factory in Bombay. At the outset Saleem himself says, "There are so many stories to tell, too many, such an excess of intertwined lives even miracles, places, rumours, so dense a commingling of the improbable and the mundane." (4) Thus in the course of the telling of these stories, Saleem takes liberties with historical dates, indulges in all kinds of extravagances, building tale within tale, and circling back from the present to the past. However, in the end, the garrulous Saleem by his sheer ingenuity binds all these stories together. He recounts episode after episode to Padma each in a distinct tone and flavour. Major historical incidents like the Jallianwallah Bagh, the moment of Independence heralding a new dawn, the wars with China and Pakistan, the Hazratbal episode and the horrendous emergency are recapitulated. Personal stories like the curious rising of Khushrov and Bhagwan, the enigmatic Mian Abdullah and old Tai, the shikara man are all told in a unique flavour. At the end, each story and episode is integrated into the main texture of the narrative.

Shame too has an episodic structure and an abundance of story within story. In the course of depicting the socio-political history of Pakistan opening with the bizarre story of the Shakil sisters in Nishapur, the narrative meanders to encompass an equally bizarre story of Sufiya, the clairvoyance of Talvar Ul haq, Naveed Hyder's unfortunate destiny and finally detours to come back to Quetta from where it all started.

Amitav Ghosh's novel *The Circle of Reason* too, has all the prominent features of the oral narrative, circular in its structure and episodic in its depiction. The novel starts with Balaram Bose and his passion for the book *Life of Pasteur*, in a small village in Bengal. The narrative moves to al-Ghazira, where Zindi dominates the story. In this section of the novel, stories abound, recreating the story of Jeevan bhai, and Nury, their meteoric rise and equally tragic fall. The last section of the novel unfolds in the distant El-Oued in the Sahara. It tells the story of a small Indian community, their hopes and aspirations in a foreign land. The novelist cleverly binds the entire structure of the novel by introducing the leit motif of the narrative, the book *Life of Pasteur*.

Similarly Upamanyu Chatterjee's novel *English, August* has story within story and is also circular in its structure. Madna has characters like Srivastav, Kumar and Govind Sathe, each with their own personal stories. Equally effective are the stories of Baba Ramanna and the Naxalites. Baba Ramanna's story is a moving example in human perseverance and compassion. The depiction of the Naxalites who have instilled a new confidence into the lives of the innocent tribals create another story in human dedication committed to creating social awareness.

Mysterious figures carrying their own stories abound in these novels as in the traditional oral narrative. Old Tai is one of the many fascinating characters in *Midnight's Children*, making a fleeting appearance but leaving an indelible mark on the reader's imagination. An enigmatic shikara man, his life is shrouded in mystery. Replete with a thorough knowledge of the hills and lakes of the picturesque valley of Kashmir, he seems to merge with the surroundings, virtually a Wordsworthian figure and a symbol of changelessness. He is the living antithesis of Oskar-Ilse-Ingrid's belief in the inevitability of change, "a quirky, enduring familiar spirit of the valley, a watery Caliban rather too fond of cheap whisky." (10) The aura of timelessness is created through his stories of associations with historically disparate figures. Old Tai claims that he "saw that Isa, that Christ, when he came to Kashmir" (11); Emperor Jehangir whose weight he knew to the tola and who he certifies "had bad breath and a good heart" (12); an officer from Iskander the Great's army burdened with a "nagging wife and an itch in the nose." (12) Even these stories appear credible coming from the mystifying figure of Old Tai. This timeless figure is contemporised when he dies tragically attempting to guard the autonomy of his beloved Kashmir.

Equally mysterious but more central to the narrative are the Shakil sisters in *Shame*. The story of the sisters Chunni, Munni and Bunny has all the ingredients of a grotesque fairytale. They are kept isolated from the outside world in a rambling decaying mansion by their eccentric father old Mr. Shakil. Completely out of touch with the outside world and having been brought up in the most repressive tradition possible, their eccentric behaviour is a natural outcome. And when the old disgruntled Mr. Shakil dies, they break free with a vengeance for just one night. The wild party thrown by them to celebrate their freedom results at a later date in the birth of a child. This child born under bizarre circumstances is ironically named Omar Khayyam Shakil. The boy is brought up in the highest traditions of "shamelessness" by his loving mothers in that edifice of shamelessness 'Nishapur.' Many years later they conceive another child under equally mysterious circumstances, who is named Babur, after the great warrior, the founder of the Mugal dynasty. However Babur grows up to become an extremist and faces a gruesome death engineered by Raza Hyder. As the narrative progresses it appears as if the three old cronies are waiting to avenge the death of their son Babur. Towards the end of the narrative, Omar Khayyam Shakil takes a fleeing Raza Hyder and his wife Biliquis to Nishapur and unwittingly delivers them into his mothers' death trap Nishapur. In Nishapur the fugitive party is engulfed in a world where time has stood still as in a grotesque fairytale. The three sisters torment Raza Hyder and his wife Biliquis in their own mysterious way. And with the gory death of Raza Hyder in the dumb waiter, they disappear as mysteriously as they had lived.

An equally mysterious character is Shombu Debnath in Amitav Ghosh's *The Circle of Reason*. A weaver by profession, he is master of the most intricate Jamdani pattern, but his talent remains unutilised due to his addiction to drink. His sudden appearances and disappearances create an aura of mystery about him. The most intriguing feature of his story is his mysterious liaison with Parboti Debi, the wife of Bhudeb Roy, the self-styled strong man of the village. The details of the relationship between the unprepossessing Shombu Debnath and Parboti Debi are deliberately left unspecified. In the end Shombu Debnath leaves Lalpukur with Parboti Debi and their child never to return again.

The story of Mast Ram in *The Circle of Reason* is an equally mysterious one. Mast Ram is a character straight out of a grotesque fairytale. Not only is his appearance grotesque but his very presence seems to bring misfortune. So strong is his jinx that in the end when he mysteriously disappears, he leaves behind a trail of death and destruction.

Mysterious characters such as Old Tai, the three Shakil sisters, Shombu Debnath and Mast Ram help to create the tinge of unreality which is intrinsic to the oral narrative tradition. Paradoxically the tradition simultaneously conveys the sense of concrete reality.

The novel of the Eighties attempts to capture the ethos of the sub-continent in all its facets—the historical, the political, the social and the psychological. In order to recreate this complex reality the novelists often make use of episodic characters so prominent in the oral narrative tradition. The turbulent political and social history of the sub-continent in the past decades is too complex to be expressed through a linear narrative. Episodic characters help to broaden out the perspectives and add valuable dimensions to the portrayal of history, helping to create an impression of the panorama of life in all its variety.

Mustasim the handsome's story in *Midnight's Children* is one of disappointed love. He is the son of the Nawab of Kif, incongruously an ancient kingdom in a modern state. The Nawab's westernized son with his beetle cut, polo-ponies, playing western songs on his guitar and his disinterest in the girls with silver nose jewellery "who fainted in the heat of his beauty" (383) was a great source of worry for him. Mustasim however falls hopelessly in love with the mysterious Jamila Singer. His love charm having failed to produce the desired results, a dejected Mustasim enlists in the army. He dies a tragi-comic death during the 1965 Indo-Pakistan war. Integrated within this story is the humorous election drama in Pakistan.

Through this episode, the novelist comments on prolongation of an absurd old way of life and more importantly on the farce of elections in a so-called modern democratic state.

The stories of Zindi, Jeevan bhai Patel and Nury in *The Circle of Reason* make interesting reading for themselves, in addition to what they have to contribute to the over-all design of the narrative. Zindi had come to al-Ghazira as a young girl. She was renowned for her beauty and was patronised by no less than the most respected Hajj Fahmy. She ran a house in al-Ghazira mostly for illegal immigrants who had come there under very trying circumstances to make a fortune. Zindi was a treasure house of stories, always ready to relate one to suit the occasion. But with the emergence of the new power structure in al-Ghazira, Zindi is quick to realise that an old way of life was coming to an end. Her attempts to buy the Durban tailoring house from Jeevan bhai proves futile due to an extraordinary turn of events. She foresees danger to the immigrants and when disaster strikes as she had feared, Zindi flees from al-Ghazira in the company of Alu, Kulfi and the child Boss. After many trials and tribulations including the traumatic rejection by her own family members, she finally comes to El-Oued in the distant Sahara. After a brief but significant stay, she embarks on one final journey with a new hope aptly symbolised by the child Boss.

Nury was named so in al-Ghazira as he was "so painfully cross-eyed . . . and in addition one of his eyes was always half shut." (246) This grotesque man, by a brilliant strategy had set up a lucrative business of egg selling, hitherto unknown in al-Ghazira. His inter-action with people during the course of his business rounds made him a man literally with an ear to the ground. His association with a local businessman Jeevan bhai inevitably sucks him into the politics of al-Ghazira. In a hilarious turn of events, his solid business crumbles when he is forced to make love to Saneyya, "then a woman of seventy five, famed in all the kingdoms for her astonishing ugliness." (255) A little later in a tragic turn of events he loses his life, when trying to escape from the tear gas shells burst by the guards of the Amir. He stumbles into the path of a camel: "the animal frenzied by the noise and the gas, bit his head clearly off his shoulder." (262)

The many faceted personality of Jeevan bhai Patel is equally absorbing. Expelled from his home in distant Durban in South Africa due to his marriage to a Bohra Muslim girl, he wanders through Mozambique, Dares salam, Zanzibar, Djibont, Perim, and Aden before he finally arrives in al-Ghazira. His shrewd business acumen takes him to the pinnacle of success. Jeevan bhai's business of dealing with guns brings him into contact with the old Malik, and in the course of time he becomes his unofficial adviser. This involvement in the politics of al-Ghazira is lucrative in terms of business but it also becomes his undoing. After one such political misadventure, he loses all that he had earned and is literally back to the point from where he had begun. "All his business and ships, his warehouses and customs and contracts were seized, only his shop in the souq and his office near the harbour were left to him." (262) Life has thus come a full circle for him. He lives an obscure existence for sometime before he once again meddles in the politics of the place. And when the police finally catch him, he hangs himself, preferring death to ignominy.

Through these two characters the novelist brings into focus the dying moments of an old regime and the emerging politics of al-Ghazira.

There are other characters that are used to broaden the reader's perception of history. Mian Abdullah in *Midnight's Children* comes to focus. The pre-Independence days were anxious days and among other things the worst was the threat of Partition looming large on the horizon. Mian Abdullah's spirited effort to thwart the designs of the Muslim Leaguers ultimately costs him his life. His sacrifice haunts the pages of history. A similar effort on the part of one Maulana Massodi is described in *The Cir-*

cle of Reason. The post-Independence is also replete with tensions of the worst kind. One such moment was the episode of the theft of the Prophet's hair from the Hazratbal mosque in Kashmir. Amitav Ghosh dwells in great detail on this episode, tracing its history. The initial shock of the theft had brought the people of Kashmir together, irrespective of religion. Maulana Massodi, a common man, had taken great courage to keep the people united in the face of such an explosive situation. He had persuaded "the first demonstrators to march with blackflags instead of green and thereby drew the various communities together in a collective display of mourning." (226) But the efforts of such men are never recognised, "forgotten and unsung today as any purveyor of sanity inevitably is in the hysteria of our subcontinent." (226) It is another sad commentary on the psyche of the sub-continent.

The story of a young boy related in *The Circle of Reason* brings to focus the militant aspect of the freedom struggle. The boy was a patriot to the core and had chosen to join a secret society, which was fighting for India's freedom. The police arrest him just before he has to undertake a major mission. Picture Singh in *Midnight's Children* is a character familiar in the oral narrative tradition. A snake charmer by profession, he uses ingenious methods to create social and political awareness, just like the 'harikatha' man in the oral narrative tradition. Similarly Khalil in *The Shadow Lines* remains an island of sanity in a world gone insane with communal passions. The simple Muslim rickshaw puller continues to show tender affection and care towards the elderly Hindu lawyer who had provided shelter to him in his time of need. As Saifuddin, a Muslim mechanic, comments:

> He's a nice fellow . . . he's a bit stupid, but he's got a good heart. That's what I always say to people—I say, he may be foolish, but he's got a good heart, otherwise why would he bother to look after the old man, a Hindu too, when he could have easily thrown him out and kept both rooms for his family. (209)

A strong human attachment develops between Khalil's family and Ukil babu, which transcend the barriers of class and creed. It is tragically befitting that they, Muslim and Hindu, should die together on the streets of Dhaka, both victims of a mindless communal mob.

Episodic characters such as Mian Abdullah, Maulana Massodi, Picture Singh and Khalil have a vital role to play in the narrative design. They symbolize the healing human touch, the sense of brotherhood, an effort to bring harmony in a sub-continent made disharmonious through warring passions, chief among them being communal discord.

Myth is an important component of the oral narrative tradition. In a country where mythological stories abound, it becomes a way of life. The use of myth presupposes a common knowledge between the narrator and the audience. In short, it acts as a verbal short hand. The novel of the Eighties, in spite of its cosmopolitan sweep, still has its strong moorings in the native tradition. However myth is not merely present to display the author's essential native attachments. Myths, like all allusions, help to enrich the texture of the narrative. They set off associations in the reader's mind, which the author exploits in order to communicate in an emphatic and compact manner. The frequent use of myth in these novels is a clear indication of their moorings in the native tradition. These myths are looked at from a new perspective in the novel of the Eighties. Almost all the important Hindu myths starting from the writing of the *Ramayana*, Rama and Sita, Ravana, Krishna, Shiva and Parvati, Vishnu and Brahma are brought into *Midnight's Children*. Saleem believes that his story to Padma is the same as the *Ramayana* dictated by Valmiki to Ganesh. Characters are not merely given mythical names but are also assigned the same functions as the mythological characters. Thus Shiva in the novel acts as both the procreator and the destroyer. And Parvati has her role to play as the consort of Shiva. A contemporary problem is used to evoke the myth of Rama and Sita. Other mythologies enter the story, like the myth of Prophet Mohammed having heard voices and also the reference to the two pronged sword Zulfikar carried by Ali, the nephew of Prophet Mohammed. And jostling for space along with all these are the myths of Samson, Scheherazade and of the Buddha. What is striking is the manner in which myths from different religions are freely used in the narrative. Two tones can be discerned, one serious and the other comic in the allusion to myths. While the myth of Ravana and the comparison of the Maha Yuga to Saleem's birth on 15 August 1947 are serious in tone; the reference to Indira's churning of matter is given comic tones when it is compared to Saleem's upset stomach. Amitav Ghosh's *The Circle of Reason* has its hero named Nachiketa after a character in mythology. In Upamanyu Chatterjee's *English, August: An Indian Story*, there are references to Krishna and Arjuna and the myth of the fisher king in the course of the protagonist's search for identity.

This two toned technique gives contemporary relevance to these myths. And it also results in the demystification of myths. The presence of myths from so many religions all contribute to the creation of a variegated and teeming multi-cultural world. Contemporary life is thus shown to be the modern man's *Ramayana* and the world his Kurukshetra.

The use of episodic characters and myth thus attach the novel of the Eighties to the oral narrative tradition. However, since the new novel and the novelists are cosmopolitan in nature, they show the inevitable impact of experimentation in fictional techniques being undertaken in new literatures all over the world. Contemporary Indian novelists thus create a fascinating mix of the old and the new by selectively and judiciously using these techniques which have found place under the canopy of the term "post-modernism." The new novel blazes a new trail in the manner in which the very old and the very new are fused, giving the Indian English novel a new dimension.

The techniques of post-modernism are subversive of established literary practices; in other words, they violate and confound traditional features and open out new perceptions and ways of interpretation. Particularly in nations with a colonial past, post-modernism has made available techniques to express the cultural plurality, the inevitable mixing of cultures. As Elleke

Boehmer says, "The novel in particular is regarded as polyphonic plurality in its authentic, street-muddied, market place form. The literature can be read as endorsing a democratic vision of multi-cultural mixing and self expression."[8] Playfulness is one of the distinguishing features of a post-modernist text. Fantasy, supernatural and myth are presented from a new perspective. The frequent authorial intrusions interrupting the story results in the violation of time sequence. This metafictional mode of intrusions is also aimed at reminding the reader that he is indeed reading fiction, an insistence on the unreliability of the narrative voice. Salman Rushdie and Amitav Ghosh employ the new conventions of magic realism to present, from a startlingly new perspective, a view of the reality of the human condition.

One of the striking features of the technique of the novel of the Eighties is the depiction of fantasy from a significantly different angle. Fantasy, unlike fairy tales, is not really about the marvellous but about man in the perilous realm; it is about the human condition. All serious fantasy is deeply rooted in human experience and is relevant to human living. It takes into account areas of experience—imaginative, sub-conscious, visionary which free the human spirit to range beyond the limits of the empirical primary world reality. In a sense, then, fantasy provides the writer with greater scope to construct his own scheme of morality, his own time structure, and his own political and social order. But at no time does apparent freedom permit the author to escape from contemporary reality. Indeed, the fundamental purpose of serious fantasy is to comment upon the real world and to explore moral, philosophical and other dilemmas posed by it. So the medium of fantasy used in fresh ways leads to an exploration of the inner workings of the personality and the fluctuating relationship between the individual and those around him. It engenders an extraordinarily enhanced perception of the nature of the primary world, which is so often imperfectly grasped until a shock is given to the senses by the introduction of the marvellous. And thus through fantasy, man does indeed enter the perilous realm and may find there both the familiar made strange and the strange made familiar.

Fantasy is used to explore new methods of expression and to expound a`deep felt sense of moral purpose. Fantasy is not escapism but a method of approaching and evaluating the real world. In the words of Ann Swinfen: "Fantasies are frequently imbued with a profound moral purpose and when set in a different historical period or more interestingly in a complete other world, display a concern for contemporary problems and offer a critique of contemporary society."[9] Fantasy is then used as a tool for social criticism. Writers find it easier to depict a dystopia, as a warning of the undesirable forms which our social and political institutions have taken or may take. Fantasy thus employs structures, motifs and the marvellous elements from its predecessors in myth, fable, legend, folk-tale and romance to drive home these points.

The use of fantasy and its associated structures is one of the techniques used by Rushdie to give expression to as complex a theme as that of *Midnight's Children*. In one of his interviews, Rushdie says that he patterned his own storytelling on "oral narration and deployed fantasy in order to be faithful to the reality of India, where millions believe in the world of the spirits."[10] *Midnight's Children* is the story of a country "which is itself a sort of dream." (137) The opening lines of the novel "I was born in the city of Bombay once upon a time" (3) sounds deceptively like a fairy tale. However as Ralph J. Crane observes, "This opening is no fairy tale, as with these opening lines Saleem Sinai's fate is tied to the fate of India."[11] As the infant Saleem Sinai and an infant India go through the grim struggle of growing up amidst a welter of events, the technique of fantasy enables Rushdie to make these unpalatable events less disconcerting. In the assessment of M.L. Pandit, "To be confronted with the truth about ourselves can be shocking but mixed with a judicious dose of fantasy and enlivened by a touch of wit and irony, it can be more palatable."[12] But fantasy used here does not take the nature of escapism, as reality which is presented at a tangent brings home the truth compelling us to come to terms with these new realities of the sub-continent. The grotesque nature of a new reality finds an appropriate manifestation in the grotesque figure of the protagonist Saleem Sinai. His birth on the stroke of the midnight hour and the various birthmarks on his face resembling the map of India establish him at the outset as a fantasy figure. Miraculous things happen to him as in a fantasy tale. Snake poison helps him to escape from the jaws of death, extraordinary powers allow him to traverse the length and breath of this vast country. Very truly, this fantasy figure takes recourse to fairy tales when given the task of having to play an important part in guiding the destiny of the new nation. As he himself says, "I buried myself in fairy tales, Hatim Tai, Batman, Superman and Sindbad." (181) This fantasy figure, when drained of an earlier power, acquires another miraculous power, the sense of smell. The Pakistan government exploits this gift to nose out insurgents in East Pakistan. As the buddha, the journey he undertakes in the Sundarbans along with the three young soldiers is through a grotesque fantasy land. The power of the widow, the perpetrator of the worst kind of humiliation on human dignity, is described in hauntingly fantastic and metaphysical terms:

> No colours except green and black the walls are green the sky is black (there is no roof) the stars are green the widow is green but her hair is black as black. The widow sits on a high chair the chair is the seat is black the widow's hair has a centre parting it is green on the left and on the right black. High as the sky the chair is green the seat is black the widow's arm is long as death its skin is green the fingernails are long and sharp and black. Between the walls the children green the walls are green the widow's arm comes snaking down the snake is green the children scream the fingernails are black they scratch the widow's arm is hunting see the children run and scream the widow's hand curls round them green and black. Now one by one the children are stifled quiet the widow's hand is lifting one by one the children green their blood is black unloosed by cutting fingernails it splashes black on walls (of green) as one by one the curling hand lifts the children high as the sky the sky is black there are no stars the

> widow laughs her tongue is green but her teeth are black. And children torn in two . . . the widow's hand comes one-byone the children scream . . . and laughing widow tearing I am rolling into little balls the balls are green and out into the night the night is black. (249-50)

There is no let-up in this sustained piece of writing. It is all related in one breath that enhances the terror. Thus a scathing criticism of the emergency is brilliantly presented through fantasy.

The gallery of extraordinary characters that fill the novel include a girl from Calcutta who has such a sharp tongue that it can inflict physical injuries on people, the Kerala boy who goes through mirrors, the Vindhyas boy who can grow taller or smaller almost at will, and the girl from Madras who can fly. And as Jean-Pierre Durix aptly observes, "The accumulation of such bizarre characters brings *Midnight's Children* closer to the oral genres . . . shows his [Rushdie's] talents as a storyteller and deliberately places him in the tradition of non-written literature."[13]

However the central fantasy that Rushdie creates is that of the midnight children's conference. It is an innovative device to represent the people of a nation who differ in language, thought and sensibility, and an attempt to unite them to fulfill a common dream. The midnight children are symbolic of the inherent potential they possess. In the words of Uma Parameswaran, "The children of this numinous hour are endowed with fantastic gifts of space-time travel and levitation, blinding beauty and genius, miracle healing and computer memory, Saleem himself had telepathic powers with which he could know other's thoughts and could communicate with those born in the same hour."[14] This aptly sums up the immense potential the people of this country possess. But very soon dissension sets in; each one is preoccupied with protecting his own interests, which in other words is the reality in this country. The midnight children's conference suggests some solutions in a decidedly tragic world, an attempt to overcome the destructive ethnic and linguistic conflicts. This fantasy creation thus has two facets. One facet is a passionate plea to unite for fulfilling a common vision and the other is the reality that holds a mirror to society. Jean-Pierre Durix remarks: "Taken in the context of India's constant threat of bursting into many different states, this novel maybe a fictional construct that aims at achieving, through the force of imagination what 'real' people have failed to do."[15] It gives a glimpse into the vision of the novelist.

The figure of Sufiya in *Shame* is undoubtedly Rushdie's masterpiece of grotesque fantasy. The development of Sufiya into a horrifying figure of mythical dimensions mirrors the traditional beauty to beast transformation so prevalent in the fantasies of world literature. Rushdie's description of Sufiya as she is gradually suffused with a surrealistic aura reaches heights of lyric intensity in certain passages:

> On all fours, the calluses thick on her palms and soles. The black hair . . . now matted around her face, enclosing it like fur; the pale skin of her mohajir ancestry burned and toughened by the sun, bearing like battle scars the lacerations of bushes, animals, her own itch-scratching nails. Fiery nails and the stink of ordure and death. (254)

This recreation of Sufiya as a fantasy figure is not merely decorative nor is it divorced from reality. Such a figure is perhaps necessary to depict the complex socio-political realities of Pakistan. The mood of the nation as it moves from a suppressed seething resentment to a violent outburst could not have been depicted as graphically in realistic terms.

Fantasy has a dual function in *Midnight's Children* and *Shame*. Firstly, it is an effect Rushdie resorts to show his adherence to the oral narrative and its ability to delight the readers. But it need not be escapist. Rushdie shows that enjoyment and serious purpose can be combined to give expression to certain compelling realities. In the case of *Midnight's Children*, these are concerned with the contemporary history of India, a long series of insensitive acts and self-centred people exploiting sectarian rivalry. In *Shame* too fantasy evokes the tragic history of Pakistan through its bizarre social customs and repressive political realities. Thus Rushdie, through his combination of semi-humorous and semi-serious tone, reflects more profoundly on the ethos of the sub-continent.

In certain episodes, the novel of the Eighties moves from fantasy onto the realms of magic realism. This term has been widely associated with the works of the Latin American novelist Gabriel Marquez and the Czechoslovakian novelist Milan Kundera, the German Gunter Grass, and Salman Rushdie. All these writers, as David Lodge says, "have lived through great historical convulsions and wrenching personal upheavals, which they feel cannot be adequately represented in a course of undisturbed realism."[16] Magic realism is identified by the introduction of marvellous and impossible events in what otherwise purports to be a realistic narrative. Without warning, the narration leaves what western critics call the conventions of verisimilitude to enter a world where everyday limitations can be infringed at will, clock time is replaced by the logic of myths, dreams or folktales. In magic realism there is always a tense connection between the real and the fantastic. Magic realism, however complex, still has clarity of statement and a tremendous power of description. As such, the impossible events function as metaphors for the extreme paradoxes of modern history.

From a study of some of the incidents represented through magic realism, it can be noticed that the novelists take recourse to this form to underline certain very important social and political issues in their novels.

The novel *Midnight's Children* uses magic realism as stated to convey the writer's concerns. Jean Pierre Durix's observation on the novels of Marquez that he "links the social and the political reality of his homeland with elements more often found in fairy tales or fantasy"[17] can also be applied to Rushdie. The death of Mian Abdullah, a liberal Muslim and a champion of unity, is shown through magic realism. This man fighting the Muslim League had a strange trait of humming. The effect of his humming "could fall low enough to give you a tooth ache, and when it rose to its heights, most feverish pitch, it had the ability of inducing erections in anyone in the vicinity." (47) This power perhaps can be attributed to his having been earlier a conjurer. The narrative alternates between the fantastic and realistic modes till the night of his gruesome killing. And as the assassins come and knock on the door the narrative abandons the realistic mode and switches to the fantastic, "Six new moons came into the room, six crescent knives held by men dressed all in black, with covered faces, and as two men held Nadir Khan, the others moved towards the humming bird." What happens then is best described in the words of the beetle chewers:

> The humming bird's hum became higher. Higher and higher, yara, and the assassin's eyes became wide as their members made tents under their robes. Then—Allah, then—the knives began to sing and Abdullah sang louder, humming high—high like he'd never hummed before. His body was hard and the long carved blades had trouble killing him; one broke on a rib, but the others quickly became stained with red. But now listen—Abdullah's humming rose out of the range of our human ears, and was heard by the dogs of the town. (49)

Some six thousand four hundred dogs made their way to the university building: "they went noisily, like an army, and afterwards their trail was littered with bones and dung and bits of hair . . the killers were so badly damaged that nobody could say who they were." (49-50)

One does not have to strain the imagination to guess the identity of the killers in spite of their covered faces. This gruesome death was soon forgotten, and this story too like many others was swept under the carpet. However the gory death of Abdullah haunts the pages of history. This death of not just a man but the death of an institution could not have been depicted in any other mode. It is a scathing indictment of narrow parochial forces riding on the waves of communal passions to hack a country into two.

Saleem's ability to become a radio transmitter and tune to

the voices of the other midnight children is another example of magic realism. His transformation to the buddha and his ordeal in the Sundarbans along with the three young soldiers is recreated through magic realism. The narrative moves in the realistic mode till the human sniffer dog Saleem joins the three young soldiers. Saleem now devoid of memory, a living vegetable, but still gifted with the sense of smell, is drafted into the army as a sniffer dog to smell out insurgents in the East wing of Pakistan. Given an old shirt to sniff, "the buddha led troops to Sheikh Mujabir's lair" (426), the most wanted man by the authorities. And as the buddha at a later stage leads the three soldiers into the Sundarbans, the narrative moves in the realistic mode for a short time. The narrative mode changes from the moment:

> One night Ayooba awoke in the dark to find the translucent figure of a peasant with a bullet hole in his heart. This was the man he had shot before going away into the Sundarbans. The peasant it appeared had now come to haunt him. A strange colourless liquid flowed out of the hole in his heart on to Ayooba's gun arm. The next morning his arm as a result was paralysed. Each night the forest sent them new punishments. Haunted by their misdeeds, which now appeared to them in the form of visions, they were soon reduced to trembling wrecks. The memories of their childhood kept coming back to them. One night Ayooba saw his mother looking down at him "offering him the delicate rice based sweets of her love; but at the moment as he reached out for the ladoos, she scurried away, he saw her climb a giant sundari—tree to sit swinging from a high branch by her tail, a white wraith like monkey with a face of his mother. This vision visited Ayooba night after night. The vision that Farooq Rashid sees is symbolic of the grinding poverty of the peasants of the sub-continent. Shaheed Dar sees a monkey that looked like an ancestor, and his father reminding him of his responsibility. All these experiences led them to a new adulthood. But the punishment was still not complete. Haunted by the voices of families, tormented

> by ghostly monkeys singing our golden Bengal "o, mother, I am poor." (437)

After the voices stopped, they were lulled into a false sense of security. It was a process of emptying them of their dreams. Finding themselves in the old temple of Kali, to their delight they find four houris. They indulge in carnal pleasures till one day they discover that they have become transparent. They now realise the trick of the forest, and salvaging a bit of their dreams; they come back to reality. However this ordeal has completely sapped them. On coming back to land they die gruesome deaths. This episode is a savage indictment of unwanted tensions modern governments create leading to expensive wars, and to a senseless loss of human lives.

In the novel *Shame* there is a constant shifting of modes in the depiction of Sufiya Zenobia. The realistic and the fantastic are clearly marked everytime she makes an appearance. The narrative settles into the magic realist mode from the moment of her escape from the attic, where she is kept chained and in a state of animated suspension. But no chains were strong enough to hold her back, and one day there was "an empty attic, broken attic, cracked beams. There was a hole in the bricked-up window. It had a head, arms, legs." (239) After this escape, her transformation to the murderous beast is complete. She now spreads terror and panic around the countryside. And when the beast finally comes to Nishapur for Omar Khayyam Shakil, there is a brief pause in the narrative when she is made human again: "the door flew open . . . she was on all four, naked coated in mud and shit, with twigs sticking to her back and beetles in her hair . . . the beast faded in her, she stood blinking stupidly, unsteady on her feet . . . but then the explosion came." (286) This powerful passage shows the novelist's method of countering the grotesque politics of a grotesque nation.

In the novel *The Circle of Reason*, Amitav Ghosh takes recourse to magic realism to show the trap that human beings have fallen into. Their lives are seen only in terms of money, everything else has little meaning. The predicament of the protagonist

Alu is a direct fall-out of the struggle between the power of money and socialist ideals. The incident of the collapse of the Star is at the outset attributed to the myth of the Sheikh of Mawali. The protagonist Alu who lies buried in the debris is miraculously saved by two sewing machines that hold a giant girder from falling on him. More miracles follow, as the narrative abandons the realistic mode and descends into magic realism. His companions who are looking for him in the debris are shocked to find him alive. And miraculously enough he also engages them in conversation quite oblivious to the fact that death was just a hair's breath away. From a hole in the debris he tells them: "I am thinking about cleanliness and dirt and the infinitely small." (235) He refuses food and water, and when he is finally rescued, it is as if he has emerged out of a deep penance. Enigmatically he tells the people of the Ras: "We shall war on money, where it all begins." (241) Alu's pronouncement is a reflection on the modern malaise of excessive love of money that seems to have taken such deep roots in the human world. It is symbolic representation of the kind of mire human beings have engulfed themselves in.

These events are a kind of metaphor for the extreme paradoxes of modern history.

Post-modernism has opened the doors to a host of new techniques through which the contemporary consciousness can be explored. Literary technique has moved away from the conventional, and freely makes use of other unconventional methods. Post-modernist writers show a willingness to experiment with non-literary techniques. This flexibility is seen in the unabashed use of the technique of the cinema. The novel of the Eighties openly uses situations and the method of the Bombay Talkies in a direct acknowledgement that it has become an intrinsic part of Indian culture. Films today are to Indian culture what folklore was to the past. Films today have permeated every aspect of life, and as a result the traditional folklore has been displaced from its position in Indian social and cultural life. It is not wrong to presume that they have become the new myths of the nation. It is a clear indication that mass culture is an inevitable part of contemporary reality. Since literature aligns itself so closely to reality, it cannot afford to ignore the emergent facts of contemporary Indian culture.

The impact of the Bombay Talkie is seen in both situations and techniques. Both these aspects are exploited to the maximum in *Midnight's Children*. Situation after situation is reminiscent of the Hindi movies. The mixed identity of the hero is a direct result of the switching of babies at birth. Thus a situation arises where the hero is born of parents of one religion and brought up by parents of another. Many Bombay films dwell on this syncretic mixture of religions in their family and social dramas. The leaving of the ransom money in an old fort by Ahmed Sinai and his business companions as instructed by the Ravana gang is a scene straight out of a Hindi movie. The hero losing his memory at a crucial stage due to an accident as it happens to Saleem Sinai after being hit by the silver spittoon is one more striking aspect. Miraculous recovery of memory again by some accident, as it again happens to Saleem when a snake in the Sundarbans bites him, completes the picture. There are other situations in the narrative dealing with secret love, and love expressed indirectly without explicit love scenes. There is a scene where an ex-husband or lover appears after a long gap. In the end as in all Hindi movies, there is a sentimental reunion between the long-lost son and the mother.

Amitav Ghosh also uses Hindi songs in both *The Circle of Reason* and *The Shadow Lines* at crucial stages in the novels. In Upamanyu Chatterjee, Hindi movie songs are constantly heard in the background.

Any narrative comes to vibrant life through an interaction of a multitude of factors. Of these the principal components are undoubtedly the quality of the author's imagination and its linguistic expression. From its inception the problem of exploring indigenous experiences in an alien tongue has troubled the Indian-English novelist. Raja Rao's *Kanthapura* is the first novel to undertake the vital task of expressing an Indian sensibility. As Raja Rao himself says in the foreword to the novel:

> One has to convey in a language that is not one's own the spirit that is one's own . . . yet English is not really an alien language to us. It is the language of our intellectual make up like Sanskrit or Persian was before . . . but not of our emotional make up. We are instinctively bilingual, many of us writing in our own language and in English. We cannot write like the English. We should not. We cannot write only as Indians. We have grown to look at the large world as a part of us. Our method of expression therefore has to be a dialect which will someday prove to be distinctive and colourful as the Irish or the American. Time alone will justify it.[18]

His contemporary Mulk Raj Anand does not exhibit the same innovativeness; nevertheless the indications of a similar awareness are to be found in the liberal use of Hindi swear words in his novels. Such attempts unintegrated with the text create an impression of artifice. R.K. Narayan and the middle generation of Indian-English novelists show a scant awareness of the problem. In this scenario one writer stands out for his daring experiments with both the form and language. G.V. Desani's novel *All about H. Hatterr*, although not fully understood nor appreciated during his time, anticipates the lines along which the novel of the Eighties could tackle the problem.

One of the significant contributions of the novel of the Eighties is to diffuse the myth of English being an alien tongue. As pointed out by Elleke Boehmer, "The postcolonial writer . . national background no longer considers English an alien tongue. The postcolonial writer is free to modify it according to his requirements."[19] In an incisive article on Rushdie's language, Agnes Scott Langland discerns a subtle political intent in subverting the traditional use of English in the new literatures of the world. She considers the Indianization of Rushdie's English as "a radical linguistic operation implanting new cultural impulses into a hitherto more narrowly ethnocentric language."[20] At this juncture it would be interesting to quote Rushdie's own views on the subject:

> The [English] language . . . needs to decolonised, to be remade in other images, if those of us use it from positions outside Anglo-Saxon are to be more than artistic uncle Toms. It is this endeavour that gives the new literatures of Africa, the Caribbean and India much of their present vitality and excitement.[21]

In another article Rushdie's views are presented forcefully. He states:

> We can't simply use the language in the way the British did; it needs remaking for our own purposes. Those of us who use English do so in spite of our ambiguity towards it. Or perhaps because of that, perhaps because we find in that linguistic struggle a reflection of other struggles taking place in the real world, struggles between the cultures within ourselves and the influences at work upon our societies. To conquer English may be to complete the process of making ourselves free.[22]

Upholding a similar viewpoint, Elleke Bohemer says, "what began in Postcolonial writing as the creolization of the English language has become a process of mass migration, transplantation and cross-fertilization. A process that is changing the nature of what was once called English Literature at its very heart."[23] Thus the authors themselves view the Indianization of language as completing the process of liberation from imperialist dominance.

It is only fair to give credit to Rushdie for giving shape to the novel of the Eighties in both form and content. The publication of *Midnight's Children* in 1981 shook the very foundations of Indian Writing in English.

Rushdie consciously took on himself the task of making the linguistic medium more flexible and suited to the requirements of the writer of the sub-continent through a process of Indianization. This process functions on several fronts—vocabulary, syntax, and use of colloquism and idiomatic turn of phrase. Almost all Indian writers prior to and contemporary have incorporated Indian words in their texts to a lesser or greater degree. Raja Rao, G.V. Desani, R.K. Narayan, Kamala Markandaya, Manohar Malgonkar, Anita Desai, Vikram Seth, Upamanyu Chatterjee are among those who have done so.

Mulk Raj Anand's English, according to Ann Lowry, is "spattered with so many Hindustani words that the western reader may feel that he is looking through frosted glass."[24] Most of these writers embed the 'native' word in the English text in such a manner as to make the meaning virtually explicit. Peter Young has aptly referred to this process as "cushioning"[25] as the reader is cushioned from a shock of being confronted with the full force of the borrowing. Rushdie frequently adopts a different tactic. His contract with the reader is founded on a less conciliatory method of presenting new words and concepts. For one thing, he rarely signals the presence of the native by the convention of using italics. Readers of Rushdie's novels are confronted with Indian words as though they ought to know them already. And if they do not, then it is up to them to find out. This happens time and again in *Midnight's Children* and *Shame*. When the meaning of the entire work is closely related to a south-Asian concept, as it is in *Shame*, Rushdie may prove more amenable towards the reader. *Shame* according to the author is the story of an imaginary land which "is not Pakistan, or not quite." (29) In this country a small, beautiful but retarded child Sufiya is the epitome of the helplessness of her Islamic sisters and of the new nation that came into existence due to the Partition of India in 1947. Sufiya is treated shamelessly by her parents who eventually marry her off to a dissolute doctor called Omar Khayyam Shakil—despite the fact that the concept of sharam is the moral prerogative on which their family life, and indeed the whole nation's life, is based. The author explains the essence of the concept:

> Sharam, that's the word, for which this paltry 'shame' is a wholly inadequate translation. Three letters, shun re mim (written naturally from right to left) plus zabar accents in-

> dicating short vowel sounds. A short word but one containing encyclopaedias of marvel. It was not only shame that his mothers forbade Omar Khayyam to feel, but also embarrassment, discomfiture, decency, modesty, shyness, the sense of having an ordained place in the world, and other dialects of emotion for which English has no counterparts. (38-39)

This foregrounding of the concept of shame by Rushdie contributes to the illumination of the theme of the novel. Tariq Rehman believes this to be the explanation why many writers "deliberately use deviant English for stylistic reasons."[26] The intrusive comment by the author that 'shame' is a wholly inadequate translation establishes the point beyond doubt. The most significant factor is that new concepts are introduced into English without a sense of self-consciousness.

There are other linguistic devices employed by Rushdie to create an Indianized hybrid English like the use of 'Babu English,' run-on words and eastern names. The characteristic features of Babu English are that it is stilted, bookish and flowery. It results in creating unfamiliar collocations and syntax, invocational forms of address and colourful terms of abuse. In Rushdie these features are used to create textual variation, and also as a means of delineating characters. Several of Rushdie's female characters use this form of English. Omar Khayyam Shakil's three mothers in *Shame* reject the English language saying: "Angrez double dutch . . . who is to understand the brains of these crazy types?" (36) and Saleem's ayah Mary in *Midnight's Children*, referring to Aadam Sinai's drunken behaviour says, "Baba, I don't know what got into your daddy now. All day sitting down there cursing curses at the dog." (243) Some of the male characters too use this form of English. Ghani the blind landowner caustically remarks about the Germany returned Dr. Aziz who is called upon to examine his daughter: "you Europe returned chappies forget certain things. Doctor sahib, my daughter is a decent girl . . . she does not flaunt her body under the noses of strange men . . . she has a terrible, a too dreadful stomach-ache." (23) The collocation "Europe returned" and the words "chappies," "doctor sahib" and "too dreadful" are all examples of Babu English.

Another typical feature of Babu English is the use of imprecations. Imprecations are used when characters give vent to strong emotions. This feature abounds in Rushdie's novels. It is interesting to list a few—O glee of female relatives in the face of unconcealable scandal. O crocodile tears and insincere pummeling of breasts (165); O endless sequence of nefarious sons of the great (333), 'O vile unhelpfulness of lickspittle uncles' (394) There are variations in moods like: 'O talismanic spittoon O beauteous lost receptacle of memories as well as spittle juice.' (448)

Another Rushdiesque linguistic marker which foregrounds Indian English is the use of run-on-words. This technique involves running together two or more words into one word. Thus such expressions as: Juicygory (77), Justlikethat (17), don'tyouthinkso (24), whatisitsname (138), everywhichthing (236) not only create a pleasing visual effect, but add a racy, colloquial effect that is characteristic of Indian speech. There are also hybrid words, rhyming words like "mummyji" and "writing shiting." In other words, the whole repertoire of English words as it is spoken in India is unfurled to entertain and provide novelty.

The names of characters in Rushdie's novels provide a clear indication of his attempt to create an Indianized variant of English. The names of most major characters and many minor characters are drawn from Muslim and Hindu sacred myths or from familiar personages or places in the past of India or the east. The majority of the names in *Midnight's Children* and *Shame* carry an aura of a mighty culture. Saleem's name in *Midnight's Children* and Sufiya's in *Shame* carry meaningful associations from the sacred texts. Omar Khayyam Shakil, Babur, Iskander Harappa have rich associations and grandeur. Rushdie's design is to create a contrast between the rich past and the present sorry state of affairs. Thus the power and the glory of the past are incorporated through language.

In short, Rushdie helps to establish a wider ethnocentric base for the English language by creating a magical and humorous Indian blend of English. His use of language strengthens the thematic critique he levels at the forces of nationalism in India and Pakistan in *Midnight's Children* and *Shame*. Rushdie's texts provide magnificent illustrations of the thesis that the novel provides an arena in which language and conflict meet. The total effect of Rushdie's techniques is to mould a vibrant prose whose positive tone makes language a bridge between cultures.

Amitav Ghosh has adopted the current practice of transcribing Hindi words without providing a glossary or even italicizing them—dalmoth and khichri appear without warning to the reader about their exotic character. The text is also interspersed with Arabic words, which gives the text a truly cosmopolitan appearance. It is another matter when the author transliterates Indian expressions into English like 'wet cat.' The British resident is called 'Goat's arse' because "whenever he spoke he made his lips into a circle of such perfection that everyone who saw him held his breath waiting for a black wonderfully rounded goat's turd to fall out." (249) There is a comic inventiveness in Amitav Ghosh's use of the language—sometimes bordering on coarseness. When the Malik fired the bazookas "the early morning crowd half dressed and unwashed, underweared and unshat, turned as one man and fled down the road with Nury in the lead." (260) Anthony Burgess best expresses Amitav Ghosh's excellence when he says, "Technically a lot of us can learn from Mr. Ghosh. It is the intelligence manifested in a brilliant handling of language that most impresses us."[27]

Upamanyu Chatterjee too shows a healthy co-existence of languages in his novels. In *English, August: An Indian Story*, he introduces interesting variations of this trend. Upamanyu Chatterjee makes a clear distinction between the English spoken in urban India and in the smaller towns. Language is used at various levels of social interaction to suit the ethos and the background. The confidence with which he uses the language at various levels thus completes the process of Indianizing English.

Thus this new generation of writers as can be seen is trailblazing. Their new vision compels us to view all countries as a part of an international unified circuit. Their approach has infused a new vitality and altered the momentum of the Indian English Novel.

In a very short span of time these writers have been hailed as world writers rather than merely being categorised as post-colonial, Commonwealth or Indian writers. While the contents of their work reveal the originality of their insight into contemporary human existence, simultaneously they are bold experimenters in language and form.

NOTES

1. Novy Kapadia, "Narrative Techniques in the Indian English," *The New Indian Novel in English: A Study of the 1980s*, ed. Viney Kirpal (New Delhi, Allied, 1990), p. 239.
2. Uma Parameswaran, "Salman Rushdie in Indo-English Literature," *Journal of Indian Writing in English*, 12.2 (1984), p. 20.
3. Walsh, pp. 120-21.
4. Irving H. Buchen, "The Aesthetics of the Supra-Novel," *The Theory of the Novel*, ed. J. Halperin (London: Penguin 1987), p. 92.
5. Salman Rushdie, Interview with David Broosk, *Helix*, 19 (1984), p. 55.
6. A. Paniker, "The Oral Narrative Tradition in Malayalam," *The Literary Criterion*, Vol. XXI, No. 1, 1986, p. 21.
7. Elleke Bohemer, *Colonial and Post-Colonial Literature* (New York: Oxford Univ. Press, 1995), p. 236.
8. Ann Swinfen, "In Defence of Fantasy," *A Study of the Genre in English and American Literature* (London: Snell, 1945), p. 2.
9. Salman Rushdie, "*Midnight's Children* and *Shame*" *Kunapipi*, 7.1 (1985), p. 12.
10. Ralph J. Crane, "The Chutnification of History," *Inventing India: A History of India in English Language Fiction* (London: Macmillan, 1992), p. 172.
11. M.L. Pandit, "Fantasy in Salman Rushdie," *The Indian Novel in English: Essays in Criticism*, ed. Ravi Nandan Sinha and R.K. Sinha (Ranchi: Ankit, 1987), p. 92.
12. Jean Pierre Durix, "The Magician of History: Salman Rushdie's

Midnight's Children," *The Writer Written: The Artist and Creation in New Literatures in English* (Connecticut: Greenwood Press, 1987), p. 125.

13. Uma Parameswaran, "Handcuffed to History: Salman Rushdie's Art," *The Perforated Sheet: Essays on Salman Rushdie's Art* (Madras: Affiliated East-West Press, 1988), p. 9.
14. Durix, p. 120.
15. David Lodge, "Magic Realism," *The Art of Fiction* (Middlesex: Penguin, 1992), p. 114.
16. Durix, p. 121.
17. Raja Rao, Foreword to *Kanthapura* (New Delhi: Orient Paperbacks, 1971).
18. Boehmer, p. 230.
19. Agnes Scott Langland, "Rushdie's Language," *English Today*, 12.1, 1996, p. 16.
20. Salman Rushdie, "The Empire Writes back with a Vengeance," *The Times*, 3 July 1982, p. 8.
21. Salman Rushdie, *Imaginary Homelands: Essays in Criticism 1981-1991* (New York: Granta/Viking, 1991), p. 17.
22. Bochmer, p. 233.
23. Ann Lowry, "Style Range in New English Literatures," *The Other Tongue: English across Cultures*, ed. Braj B. Kachru (Urbana and Chicago: University of Illinois Press, 1992), p. 288.
24. Peter Young, "Tradition, Language and the Reintegration of Identity in West African Literature in English," *The Critical Evaluation of African Literature*, ed. Edgar White (London: Heinemann, 1973), p. 40.
25. Tariq Rehman, "Linguistic Deviation as a Stylistic Device in Pakistani English Fiction," *The Journal of Commonwealth Literature*, 25.1, 1990, p. 9.
26. Anthony Burgess, Rev. of *The Shadow Lines*, *The New York Times Book Review*, 12.5 (1988), p. 40.

Conclusion

This study has attempted to bring out the originality stamped on every aspect of the novel of the eighties. Originality is seen in the reformulation of old ideas and the discovery of new ones. The five major novels discussed in the book bear this out. The connection between the individual and his relation to history and political circumstances that frame his life is not new to Indian English novel. However the originality of perception which the authors bring to this theme gives it an entirely new and relevant form. In a country riddled with communal tensions and vested political interests the individual can no longer afford to be a mere bearer or sufferer of history. It requires of him a determined, even if unsuccessful, effort to combat the dehumanising forces of such circumstances. The novel of the Eighties by interrogating history gives fiction the relevance for the contemporary times. It perhaps suggests the consciousness required in creating a new and more humane order.

The theme of the search for identity has been shown to be reformulated in the novel of the Eighties, again in keeping with the demands of the changed times. The extension of cultural frontiers, internationalism and cosmopolitanism are undeniable parts of the new reality. The novel of the Eighties is embedded in the new trans-cultural, trans-continental consciousness. Hence the former spiritual quest and East-West cultural encounters are rendered obsolete and are replaced by the search for a cosmopolitan identity. Consequently, the new protagonists have been shown to be cultural travellers in search for an emotional bondage rather than a geographical one. The protagonists of *Midnight's Children, Shame, The Circle of Reason, The Shadow Lines* and *English, August* are all on the move. While Saleem wanders through the subcontinent, Alu's movement is trans-continental. The unnamed narrator of *The Shadow Lines* moves between India and London. Their constant endeavour is to forge links with people belonging to different cultures irrespective of place. The new protagonist is a prominent departure from the traditional image of the fictional hero—unromantic, occasionally grotesque but still retaining a warm humanity in spite of the pressures of contemporary existence.

A similar combination of traditional devices reformulated and startlingly new ones discovered functions on the level of technique. As in theme it is this reformulation which has given the novel of the Eighties its relevance to contemporary times. The oral narrative with its use of myth, episodicity and story within story is interfaced with magic realism, movie techniques and a new vibrant use of the English language. It is only such a technique that can expound the complex consciousness of a world functioning on radically different paradigms. This transformation of theme and technique has transported the hitherto insular Indian English novel to the broader frontiers of the new literatures of the world. The works of Salman Rushdie, Amitav Ghosh and Upamanyu Chatterjee have taken the Indian English novel to the highest echelons of world literature.

The most valuable insight that has been gained through this study is the redeeming power of the human touch. Protagonist after protagonist has been shown to impose a degree of control over circumstances which threaten to swamp his spirit through this fundamental human instinct. All the novels studied bear testimony to this aspect. Saleem Sinai in *Midnight's Children* bemoans the absence of compassion and holds it responsible for his predicament. Omar Khayyam Shakil in *Shame* breaks free from his shackles of shamelessness when he shows compassion towards Sufiya Zenobia. Alu in *The Circle of Reason* is witness to the human touch and compassion shown by Mrs. Verma. The unnamed narrator in *The Shadow Lines* sees compassion in May Price and the lack of it in the subcontinent which results in the death of Tridib. Agastaya Sen's life in *English, August* takes a new turn when in a decisive action he shows his human warmth by alleviating the suffering of the hapless tribals. It is this aspect that significantly changes the lives of all the protagonists. The demands of contemporary existence do not call for any sophisticated intellectual solutions. The solution propounded in the novel of the Eighties is startling in its simplicity particularly when contrasted with the complexity of its technique. Underlying the virtuoso performance and pyrotechnics is a moving emphasis on the necessity of supporting human relationships and a mutual human concern and caring. It is this factor that can act as a stabilising and binding force in an increasingly fragmented world. What emerges from this study is this insight that has not been sufficiently recognised. In the surrounding gloom it is these novels that hold out a ray of hope through their positive vision. The emergence of this perception gives the novel of the Eighties a unique relevance. Another valuable insight that has been gained is that the new protagonists in the search for identity are constantly on the move compared to the static world of the past in the earlier novels. Identity is established through interaction and association with other human beings. The new protagonists look ahead and move forward to come to terms with the complex realities of modern life rather than taking recourse to withdrawal or retreat as it happens in the earlier novels. The novel of the Nineties continues this tradition. This line of study bears further investigation. And it is hoped that this present book will have suggested the challenge of such a study to potential researchers.

Bibliography

Primary Sources

Rushdie, Salman. *Grimus*. London: Grafton Books, 1975.
______. *Midnight's Children*. 1980. New York: Avon Books, 1982.
______. *Shame*. 1983. Calcutta: Rupa.
______. *The Jaguar Smile: A Nicaraguan Journey*. 1988. New York: Penguin.
Ghosh, Amitav. *The Circle of Reason*. 1986. New Delhi: Roli Books International.
______. *The Shadow Lines*. 1988. New Delhi: Ravi Dayal Publisher. 1992.
Chatterjee, Upamanyu. *English, August: An Indian Story*. 1988. New Delhi: Rupa, 1994.

Secondary Sources

Allen, Walter. *Reading a Novel*. London: Phoenix House, 1940.
Bohemer, Elleke. *Colonial and Postcolonial Literature*. New York: OUP, 1995.
Brennan, Timothy. *Salman Rushdie and the Third World*. London: Hamilton, 1989.
Buchen, Irving H. "The Aesthetics of the Supra Novel." *The Theory of the Novel*. Ed. J. Halperin.
Burgess, Anthony. *All About H. Hatterr*. By G.V. Desani, London: The Bodley Head, 1970.
Chandra, Suresh. "Metaphor of Shame: Salman Rushdie's Fact Fiction." *Culture and Criticism: New World Literature Series*, ed. Suresh Chandra. New Delhi: B.R., 1987.
Couto, Mario. "The Search for Identity." *The Eye of the Beholder: Indian Writing in English*. Ed. Maggie Butcher. London: Commonwealth Institute, 1983.
Crane, Ralph J. *Inventing History: History of India in English Language Fiction*. London: Macmillan, 1992.
Cronin, Richard. *Imagining India*. London: Macmillan, 1989.
Dass, Veena Noble and R.K. Dhawan, ed. *Fiction of the Nineties*. New Delhi: Prestige, 1994.
Desai, Anita. "Where Cultures Clash by Night." *Book World: Contemporary Literary Criticism*, Vol. 23. Detroit: Gale Research Co., 1983.
Dhawan, R.K., ed. *Commonwealth Fiction*. New Delhi: Classical, 1988.
______ *Indian Literature Today*. Vol. 1: Drama and Fiction. New Delhi: Prestige, 1994.

______. *The Novels of Salman Rushdie.* New Delhi: Indian Society for Commonwealth Studies, 1992.

______. *Three Contemporary Novelists.* New Delhi: Classical, 1985.

Dhawan, R.K., et. al, ed. *Recent Commonwealth Literatures.* New Delhi: Prestige, 1981.

Dingwaney, Anuradha. "Author(izing) *Midnight's Children* and *Shame*: Salman Rushdie's Construction of Authority." *Reworlding: The Literature of the Indian Diaspora.* Ed. Nelson Emmauels. Westport: Greenwood, 1992.

Durix, Jean, Pierre. *The Writer Written: The Artist and Creation in New Literatures in English.* Connecticut: Greenwood Press, 1987.

Gasiorek, Andrej. *Post War British Fiction: Realism and After.* London: Edward Arnold, 1995.

Gupta, G.S. Balarama. *Studies in Indian Fiction in English.* Gulbarga: JIWE, 1987.

Islam, Shamsul. "Rushdie and Political Commitment: A Study of *Midnight's Children* and *Shame.*" *Literature and Commitment.* Ed. Govind Narain Sharma. Toronto: TSAR, 1988.

Iyengar, K.R. Srinivasa. *Indian Writing in English.* New Delhi: Sterling, 1990.

Kamaluddin, Sabiha. "*Midnight's Children* as a Truncated Narrative." *Critical Responses: Commonwealth Literature.* New Delhi: Sterling, 1993.

Kerr, David. "History and the Possibilities of Choice: A Study of Anita Desai's *Baumgartner's Bombay,* Upamanyu Chatterjee's *English, August* and Shashi Deshpande's *That Long Silence.*" *Indian Women Novelists.* Set 1, Vol. 1. Ed. R.K. Dhawan. New Delhi: Prestige, 1991.

Kırpal, Vinay, ed. *The Third World Novel of Expatriation: A Study of Emigre Fiction by Indian, African and Caribbean Writers.* New Delhi: Sterling, 1989.

______. *The New Indian Novel in English: A Study of the 1980s.* New Delhi: Allied, 1990.

Kriplani, Krishna. *Indian Literature: A Panoramic Glimpse.* Bombay: Nirmal Sadanand, 1969.

Kundera, Milan. *The Art of the Novel.* Trans. Linda Aster. New Delhi: Rupa, 1995.

Lodge, David. *The Art of Fiction.* Middlesex: Penguin, 1992.

Lowry, Ann. "Style Range in New English Literatures." *The Other Tongue: English Across Cultures.* Ed. Braj B. Kachru. Urbana and Chicago: Univ. of Illinois Press, 1992.

Mathur, O.P. "A Metaphor of Reality: A Study of the Protagonist of *Midnight's Children.*" *Indian English Literature since Independence.* Ed. Ayyappa K. Paniker. New Delhi: Indian Association for English Studies, 1991.

Mattoo, Neeraja. "Indianness in *Midnight's Children*: Rushdie's View of an 'Amnesiac Nation'?" *The Indian Novel in English: Essays and Criticism.* Ed. Ravi Nandan Sinha and R.K. Sinha. Ranchi: Ankit, 1987.

Mukherjee, Meenakshi. *Twice Born Fiction.* New Delhi: Arnold Heinemann, 1971.

Murphy, Michael. *Grefin the Kingdom.* New York: Dell, 1972.

Naik, M.K. "The Life of Fragments: The Fate of Identity in *Midnight's Children* English Literature." *Studies in Indian Literature*. New Delhi: Sterling, 1983.

______. *Gandhi in Literature*. Mysore: Univ. of Mysore, 1971.

Narasimhaiah, C.D. "Spurious Reputations: Vikram Seth, Salman Rushdie and Shashi Tharoor." *Essays in Commonwealth Literature: Heirloom of Multiple Heritage*. Ed. C.D. Narasimhaiah. New Delhi: Pencraft, 1995.

______. *Kanthapura: An Analysis. Critical Essays on Indian Writing in English*. Ed. M.K. Naik. Dharwar: Karnatak Univ., 1968.

Nietzsche, Friedrich. *On the Uses and Disadvantages of History for Life*. Trans. R.J. Hollingdale. Cambridge: Cambridge Univ. Press, 1983.

Pandit, M.L. "Fantasy in Salman Rushdie." *The Indian Novel in English: Essays in Criticism*. Ed. Ravi Nandan Sinha and R.K. Sinha. Ranchi: Ankit, 1987.

Parameswaran, Uma. *The Perforated Sheet: Essays on Salman Rushdie's Art*. Madras: Affiliated East-West Press, 1988.

Pathak, R.S. ed. Indian *Fiction in English: Problems and Promises*. New Delhi: Northern Book Center, 1990.

______. *Quest for Identity in Indian English Writing*. New Delhi: Bahri, 1992.

______. *Recent Indian Fiction*. New Delhi: Prestige, 1994.

Rao, Madhusudhan, M. *Salman Rushdie's Fiction: A Study*. New Delhi: Sterling, 1992.

Rao, K. Raghavendra. "The Novel as History as Chutney: Unriddling Salman Rushdie's *Midnight's Children*." *Perspectives on Indian Fiction in English*. Ed. M.K. Naik. New Delhi: Abhinav, 1985.

Reddy, P. Bayappa. *Studies in Indian Writing in English*. New Delhi: Prestige, 1990.

Reddy, K. Venkata. *Critical Studies in Commonwealth Literature*. New Delhi: Prestige, 1994.

Rockwell, Joan. *Fact in Fiction: The Use of Literature in the Systematic Study of Society*. London: Routledge and Kegan, 1974.

Syal, Pushpinder. *Structure and Style in Commonwealth Literature*. New Delhi: Vikas, 1994.

Walsh, William. *Indian Literature in English*. Harlow: Longman, 1990.

Articles in Journals, Magazines and Newspapers

Afzal-Khan, Fawzia. "Post Modernist Strategies of Liberation in the Works of Salman Rushdie." *Journal of South Asian Literature*, 23.1 (1998): 137-45

Alam, Fakrul. "Travelling in the West: the Writing of Amitav Ghosh." *The Journal of Commonwealth Literature*, 31.1 (1996).

Ali, Siddiq. "*Midnight's Children* as Historiography." *Osmania Journal of English Studies*, 25 (1989), 130-39.

Ali, Tariq. "Where is Pakistan Going?" *The Illustrated Weekly of India*, 16 Oct. 1983.

Amanuddin, Syed. "The Novels of Salman Rushdie: Mediated Reality as Fantasy." *World Literature Today*, 63.1 (1989): 42-45.

Banerjee, Ashutosh. "Narrative Techniques in *Midnight's Children*." *The Commonwealth Review*, 1.2 (1990): 23-32.

Batty, Nancy E. "The Art of Suspense: Rushdie's 1001 (Mid-) Nights." *Ariel*, 18.3 (1987): 49-65.

Bhatt, Indira. "*Shame*: A Thematic Study." *The Commonwealth Review*, 1.2 (1990): 64-70.

Brennan, Timothy. "Shames Holy Book." *The Journal of Indian Writing in English*, 16.2 (1988): 211-227.

Brigg, Peter. "Salman Rushdie's Novels: The Disorder in Fantastic Order." *World Literature Written in English*, 27.1 (1987): 119- 130.

Chandra, Suresh. "The Metaphor of *Shame*: Rushdie's Fact Fiction." *The Commonwealth Review*, 1.2 (1990): 77-84.

Chausse, Griffith A. "A Textual Unicorn: Identity and Islamic Reference in Salman Rushdie's *Shame*." *The Toronto South Asian Review*, 8.3 (1990): 17-27.

Clifford, James. "The Transit Lounge of Culture." *Times Literary Supplement*, 4596, 3 May 1991: 7-8.

Cook, Rufus. "Place and Displacement in Salman Rushdie's Work." *World Literature Today*, 68.1 (1994): 23-28.

Dharkar, Deval. "Discussion on *Midnight's Children*." *New Quest*, 36 (1982) 350-351.

Dixon, Robert. "Travelling in the West: The Writing of Amitav Ghosh." *The Journal of Commonwealth Literature*, 31.1 (1996): 8.

Ezekiel, Nissim. *Indian Post*, 21 August 1988.

Flaganan, Kathleen. "The Fragmented Self in Salman Rushdie's *Midnight's Children*." *Commonwealth Novel in English*, 5.1 (1992): 39-45.

Fletcher, M.D. "Rushdie's *Shame* as Apologue." *The Journal of Commonwealth Literature*, 21.1 (1986): 123

Hollington, Michael. "Salman Rushdie's *Shame*." *Meanjin Quarterly*, 3 September (1984): 405.

Iyer, Pico. "The Empire Writes Back." *Time International*, 8 Feb 1993: 49.

Jaidev. "Salman Rushdie: The Indian Postmodernist." *Punjab Journal of English Studies*, 2 (1987): 29-38.

Joshi, B.K. "It May be Long, but it is not overwritten." *The Times of India*, 1 November 1981: 8.

Jussawalla, Feroza. "Beyond Indianness: The Stylistic Concerns of *Midnight's Children*." *The Journal of Indian Writing in English*, 12.2 (1984): 26-47.

Kamaluddin, Sabiha. "*Midnight's Children*: History as Truncated Narrative." *Osmania Journal of English Studies*, Vol. 25 (1989): 124-29.

Kortenaar, Neil, Ten. "*Midnight's Children* and the Allegory of History." *Ariel*, 26.2 (1995): 41.

Kothandaraman, Bala. "Circular Reasoning: Amitav Ghosh's Rhetoric." *Osmania Journal of English Studies*, 25 (1989): 151-158.

Krishnaswamy, Revathi. "Mythologies of Migrancy: Postcolonialism, Postmodernism and the Politics of (Dis)location." *Ariel*, 26.1 (1995): 125-146.

Langland, Scott, Agnes. "Rushdie's Language." *English Today*, 12.1 (1996) 16.

Mathur, O.P. "Sense and Sensibility in *Shame*." *The Commonwealth Review*, 1.2 (1990): 85-93.

Merivale, Patricia. "Saleem Fathered by Oskar: Intertextual Strategies in *Midnight's Children* and *The Tin Drum*." *Ariel*, 21.3 (1995): 7-45.

Mishra, Vijay. "Postcolonial Differend: Diasporic Narratives of Salman Rushdie." *Ariel*, 26.3 (1995): 7-45.

Narayan, Shyamala. "The Structure of Amitav Ghosh's *The Circle of Reason*." *The Literary Criterion*, 14.1-2 (1988): 43-55.

Oomen, Susan. "Fictional Intent in Rushdie's *Shame*." *The Literary Criterion*, 20.2 (1985): 36-41.

Painter, Andrew. "The Significance of 'Ami' in *Circle of Reason* in a Given Context." *Odyssey: International Journal for Literature and Philosophy*, 1 (1996): 33-46.

Paniker, A. "The Oral Narrative Tradition in Malayalam." *The Literary Criterion*, XXI, 1 (1986): 21.

Parameswaran, Uma. "Saleem Sinai and India in Rushdie's *Midnight's Children*." *The Toronto South Asian Review*, 1.2 (1982): 52-61.

Price, David W. "Salman Rushdie's Use and Abuse of History in *Midnight's Children*." *ARIEL: A Review of International English Literature*, 25.2 (1994) 93.

Rahman, Tariq. "Politics in the Novels of Salman Rushdie." *The Commonwealth Review*, 1.2 (1990): 102-117.

Ram, Uma. "The Narrator's Development in Amitav Ghosh's *The Shadow Lines*." *Indian Scholar*, 14.2 (1992): 49-57.

Rao, Bhargavi P. "Amitav Ghosh's *The Shadow Lines*." *Osmania Journal of English Studies*, 25 (1989): 159-163.

Rao, K. Damodar. "Silence as Possible Mode of Response in Amitav Ghosh's *The Shadow Lines*." *Kakatiya Journal of English Studies*, Vol. XIII (1993): 83.

Rath, Surya Prasad. "Narrative Design in Salman Rushdie's *Shame*." *The Journal of Indian Writing in English*, 13.2 (1985): 27-38.

Raykar, Meenakshi. "The Intellectual in a State of 'Anomy': *No Longer at Ease* and *English, August: An Indian Story*." *New Quest*, (1992): 92.

Rehman, Tariq. "Linguistic Deviation as a Stylistic Device in Pakistani English Fiction." *The Journal of Commonwealth Literature*, 25.1 (1990): 9.

Ross, Robert L. "The Emerging Myth: Partition in the Indian and Pakistani Novel." *ACLALS Bulletin*, 7.4 (1986): 3.

Rushdie, Salman "The Empire Writes back with a Vengeance." *The Times*, 3 July 1982: 8.

Sengupta, C. "Upamanyu Chatterjee's *English, August*: Metaphor of Contemporary Youth's Quest of Self-Realisation." *The Commonwealth Review*, 5.1 (1993-94): 110-21.

Shepherd, Ron. "*Midnight's Children* as Fantasy." *The Commonwealth Review*, 5.2 (1990): 33-43.

Singh, Sushila. "Salman Rushdie's Novels: From Fantasy to Reality." *The Commonwealth Review*, 1.1 (1989): 111-123.

Srinath, C.N. "The Writer as Historical Witness: Khushwant Singh's *Train to Pakistan* and Chaman Nahal's *Azadi*." *The Literary Criterion*, 25.2 (1990): 60.

Srivastava, Aruna. "The Empire Strikes Back: Language and History in *Shame* and *Midnight's Children*." *Ariel*, 20.4 (1989): 70.

Swann, Joseph. "East is East and West is West?: Salman Rushdie's *Midnight's Children* as an Indian novel." *World Literature Written in English,* 26.2 (1986): 353-362.

Syed, Mujeebuddin. "*Midnight's Children* and its Indian Contexts." *The Journal of Commonwealth Literature,* 29.2 (1994): 95-108.

Interviews and Reviews

Ball, John Clement. "An Interview with Salman Rushdie," *The Toronto South Asian Review,* 10.1 (1991): 30-37

Dharkar, Rani. "An Interview with Salman Rushdie," *New Quest,* 42, Nov.-Dec. 1983: 357-360.

Rushdie, Salman. Interview "Author from Three Countries," By Michael J. Kaufman. *New York Book Review,* 13 Nov. 1983: 3.

______. Interview by David Broosk, *Helix,* 19 (1984): 55.

______. Interview by Gordon Wise. *Gentleman,* Feb. 1984: 59.

______. Interview by Anna Rutherford. *Kunapipi,* 4.2 (1982): 24.

Blabber, Ron. "Darkness and Hope," Rev. of *Midnight's Children, CRNLE Reviews Journal,* No. 2, 1982: 33-35.

Burgess, Anthony. Rev. of *The Circle of Reason, Times Book Review,* 6 July: 6.

Couto, Mario. Rev. of *Shame, Kunapipi,* 6.2 (1984): 121-124.

Doctor, Geetha. Rev. of *English, August, Literature Alive,* 3.2, 1989: 18-19.

Ezekiel, Nissim. "The Comfortable Tiredness of Intoxication," Rev. of *English, August, Sunday Observer,* 31 July 1988.

Jewison, D.B. Rev. of *Shame, The Toronto South Asian Review,* 2.3 (1964): 79.

Karnad Girish. "Worlds within Worlds," Rev. of *The Shadow Lines, Indian Express Magazine,* 18 Dec. 1988: 5.

Kaul, K.R. "A Sealed Chutney Bottle," Rev. of *Midnight's Children, Indian Book Chronicle,* 11.11-12 (1986): 248.

King, Bruce. Rev. of *The Rushdie File, World Literature Today,* 64.3 (1990): 529-530.

Lal, Vinay. "Enjoyable Reading," Rev. of *English, August, Indian Literature,* No. 3 (1990): 155-162.

Mukherjee, Meenakshi. "Dissolving Divides: Inter-weaving Strands of Memory and Imagination," Rev. of *The Shadow Lines,* by Amitav Ghosh, *India Today,* 13.18 (1988), 158.

______. "Irrelevant, Exuberant and Metaphoric," Rev. of *Midnight's Children, Indian Book Chronicle,* 6.23 (1981): 381-382.

Nazareth, Peter. Rev. of *Midnight's Children, World Literature Written in English,* 21.1 (1982): 169-71.

Rao, Vimala Rama. Rev. of *English, August, The Literary Criterion,* 27.4 (1992): 78-79.

Wasi, Jehanara. Rev. of *The Circle of Reason, Indian Horizons,* 36.1-2 (1987), 53.